childhood treasures

CAROLINE ZOOB

childhood treasures
handmade gifts for babies and children

PHOTOGRAPHY BY
CAROLINE ARBER

RYLAND
PETERS
& SMALL
LONDON NEW YORK

Senior designer Sally Powell

Commissioning editor Annabel Morgan

Editor Sophie Bevan

Location research Emily Westlake

Production Deborah Wehner

Art director Gabriella Le Grazie

Publishing director Alison Starling

Illustrations Lizzie Sanders

*For my husband Jonathan, our nieces
Ana and Katerina, and our very dear
small friends Sebastian, Freddie,
Imogen, and William.*

First published in the United States
in 2003. This paperback edition first
published in 2006 by
Ryland Peters & Small, Inc.
519 Broadway, 5th Floor
New York, NY 10012
www.rylandpeters.com

10 9 8 7 6 5 4 3 2 1

Text © Caroline Zoob 2003, 2006
Design and photographs
© Ryland Peters & Small 2003, 2006

ISBN-10: 1-84597-216-3
ISBN-13: 978-1-84597-216-5

The original edition of this book was
cataloged as follows:

Library of Congress Cataloging-in-
Publication Data:
Zoob, Caroline.
 Childhood treasures : handmade
gifts for babies and children /
Caroline Zoob ; photography by
Caroline Arber.
   p. cm.
 ISBN 1-84172-478-5
 1. Handicraft. 2. Children's
paraphernalia. I. Title.
 TT157.Z66 2003
 745.5--dc21
                    2003010024

Printed and bound in China

Important note:
Measurements for the projects in
this book are given in imperial and
metric. Conversions are not exact.
Always follow **either** the imperial
or the metric measurements when
making up a project.

contents

introduction

One of the great pleasures derived from writing this book has been to talk to people about their most loved childhood toys and possessions. As I was seeking out inspirational treasures with which to illustrate the book, flea-market vendors and friends started to reminisce about the blankets, clothes, teddy bears, and dolls they remembered from their childhoods. Some people still had these treasures, stored in suitcases in the attic, and unearthed them for me to look at and use. Mostly, their childhood toys were now just memories, but very clear memories, and it was touching to hear people well into middle age talk about the wardrobe of knitted dolls' dresses their aunt made for them, or the set of wooden soldiers a grandfather had carved.

Grown up, most of us have memories of particular gifts or presents we received as children, and the excitement they caused. At the time, we probably didn't notice or care

Children appreciate beautiful things: they like to look at them and use them every bit as much as adults. An heirloom piece is such because of its place in a child's memory as much as for the work and love that has gone into it. This nineteenth-century sailor's chest, lined with floral wallpaper by the sailor's mother and decorated with a picture of his ship, would make a memorable toy chest for a little boy. A pretty little doll's teacup, much used in childhood, makes a delightful grown-up ornament.

whether the gifts were handmade or purchased. People choose to make gifts with their own hands for various reasons: some because their funds are limited, some because they have particular skills. Common to both is the love for a particular child, which makes them spend hours carving, painting, stitching, or knitting to create a unique gift. The handmade gift is appreciated even more today, when we are surrounded by a bewildering array of things to buy for children, and time is everyone's most precious commodity. Hopefully this book will inspire people to use a little of that time to think about making things for the children in their lives.

Of course, a child who wants a computer game or football shirt with every fiber of his being is not going to be as happy with an intricate quilt or a set of carved animals. The game, shirt, or its equivalent has to be bought, however reluctantly.

Not only are old toys and clothes lovely to play with, they can also provide the inspiration for making your own projects. The graphic shape of the figures on this little pull-along toy **(near right)** makes the most charming painted frieze for a treasure box (see pages 82–83) or nursery wall, or could be transferred onto fabric and appliquéd across a window shade or valance.

However, the purchased presents can be offset with the occasional small handmade or vintage present that will last a lifetime. I was greatly encouraged when I asked a small friend of mine what he would like for his sixth birthday, fully expecting him to suggest some lurid and noisy piece of high technology. I was astounded and deeply touched by his reply, given immediately and without guile: "Perhaps a quilt?" On her fourth Christmas Day, my eldest niece, surrounded by a sea of colorful presents and wrapping, declared that her favorite present was an old painted box that had been filled with new crayons, paints, and modeling clay.

It is so disheartening when people look at something I have made and say "Oh, but that's too good for a child." Nothing is too precious or beautiful for a child. Historically, some of the most exquisite textile pieces were made to celebrate the birth of a child, to cover them while they

slept, or to decorate their rooms. We can stitch into cloth the inexpressible joy brought into life by children, whether our own or those of others. It is this love, for the child, for the child's family, that goes into something made by hand which makes it such a cherished gift. Children are able to recognize that something is precious, a thing you have to treasure and be careful with. Arguably, it is only in handling delicate, fragile things that children learn the need for physical restraint.

On my sixth birthday, we were living in the Cameroons, a magical place in which to grow up. My English picture books were full of wondrous rocking horses, and I longed for one on which to fulfill all my fantasies of riding through the uncharted jungle. Even to my eyes, it was clear that the small town of Bota in 1965 was sadly lacking in toy stores and my best hopes lay with Santa Claus in a few months' time. However,

Antique stores are very good sources of vintage treasures with which to add character and charm to a nursery or playroom. Some will be too fragile to use every day, but many are as robust as they were when new, and the peeling paint and worn air only adds to their attractiveness. Many dealers make stuffed toys and little bears from antique linens and dress them in vintage fabric clothes. The samplers (near left) were designed and made by a Dutch grandmother for each of her two grandsons and have become precious family heirlooms.

on my birthday, my parents led me, blindfolded, onto the veranda that ran around the house. The blindfold was removed to reveal a most beautiful, dappled-gray rocking horse with a painted red saddle, which my father had made and painted himself. No other rocking horse since has captivated me as much, and the memory of it is one of my childhood treasures. We could not bring it home with us, and I like to think that perhaps it has survived, its paint worn and its mane a bit tatty, a much-loved toy somewhere in the Cameroons. I think of it every time I walk around an antique mall and see hand-painted toys obviously made by fathers and grandfathers. Pieced together with often rudimentary handyman skills using old cigar boxes and bits of plywood, they possess more character than any purchased toy. It is all the more touching that they have been made with a particular beloved child in mind.

welcome to the world

No matter how cynical and materialistic our world becomes, a new baby, even glimpsed momentarily snoozing on a parental shoulder in a crowded supermarket, revives our sense of the wonder of life. Making a gift for a baby is an expression of love, not only for the baby, but also for the family it is born into. Stitch favorite sayings, lines from a hymn sung at the parents' wedding, or even family names onto patchwork crib quilts, cozy blankets, or a cross-stitch sampler.

The text on the heart reads:

To LOVE and CHERISH

FOREVER and EVER

LOVE is BEST

Chlöe

LOVE the Giver

It is ONLY with the HEART one can SEE RIGHTLY

Bound by the SAME

HEART KNOT

The inclusion of text lends significance to a piece of patchwork. Here I have used my favorite quotations about love—all kinds of love—in a patchwork heart to decorate the bedroom of a little girl. Keep a rag bag of fabrics and textile treasures so you have a hoard from which to assemble pieces.

there is a lift of the heart when we hear that a child has been born, and an impulse to mark the occasion

Years before friends started to have children, I was impressed by a Dutch friend who made a cross-stitch sampler to celebrate the birth of each of her grandsons. At that time I had picked up a needle only to sew on buttons, and I was struck by the amount of time and effort she was putting into these intricate gifts. It was clear that for her these tiny stitches were an intensely personal expression of her delight in becoming a grandmother. Handmade things that have survived great periods of time, especially those which have remained in the same family from generation to generation, are very inspiring. The source of this inspiration is not only the skill, but also the thought that the same mixture of love and excitement welcomes in each generation of children. So, even if you are currently without the benefit of handmade family heirlooms, the arrival of a new child is an opportunity to create one. If you do not have your own children, then you have all the more time to make heirlooms for someone else's child. The things you make may become the fragile and precious treasures of the next century.

Quilters used to keep "piece bags" containing scraps their mothers and grandmothers had placed there. The antique quilts made from them are a compendium of family history, each person symbolized by a bit of textile. This idea is wonderfully celebrated in the anonymous poem on this page (see right) called *The Hooked Rug*.

One of the most beautiful baby quilts I have ever seen was pieced together in log-cabin style around squares, using a miscellany of homespun fabrics, scraps of family history. In each square was an appliquéd heart across which was embroidered the name of each family member and their relationship to the child it was made for. Folk art is also extremely inspiring. The naïve and generous

"The Hooked Rug"

I am the family wardrobe, best and worst
Of all generations, from the first;
Grandpa's Sunday-go-to-meetin' coat,
And the woollen muffler he wore at his throat;
Grandma's shawl, that came from Fayal;
Ma's wedding gown, three times turned and once let down,
Which once was plum but now turned brown;
Pa's red flannels, which made him itch;
Pants and shirts; petticoats and skirts;
From one or another, but I can't tell which,
Tread carefully, because you see, if you scuff me,
You scratch the bark of the family tree.

The quilt **(opposite)** was inspired by the birth of my godson. Favorite lines of poetry, wishes and hopes were embroidered around symbols of love, family life, and adventures to come, the stitches flying into the fabrics in the excitement of his arrival.

We may not indulge in afternoon tea laid out on embroidered traycloths any more, but those traycloths can be recycled. The person who embroidered the flowers on these sails **(right)** would surely rather they were looked at by a little boy in his nursery nearly a century later, than think of them lying in a heap on a flea market booth—intact but unappreciated. These sunflowers **(left)** were found on a stained tablecloth full of holes, but have been brought back to life accompanying the parade of vintage elephants on this quilt.

17

Cz

A sailboat picture **(left)** made from antique linens and mattress covers has been personalized with the name and birth date of the little boy named Max who inspired its creation.

A wonderful vintage pond yacht **(opposite and below)** has been given new linen sails with a tiny applique patch and the name and birth date of a little boy named Sebastian. Hardly any stitching was required to make an unusual gift, which will be as decorative in his study when he is grown up as it is in his nursery.

shapes lend themselves to reproduction in many forms, but particularly in fabric. Hearts, birds, stars, moons, and simple flowers are all shapes with many resonances for use on a child's quilt.

There is no doubt that patchwork is time-consuming, so if your time is short, you can always make a bought quilt or blanket more personal by adding a little embroidery or appliqué of your own. That is the only problem with handmade presents for new babies: it is hard to get started before they arrive safely into the world, and then, once they arrive, the pressure is on to complete the gift before they have grown too big for it!

Anyway, a present for a new baby does not have to be stitched! Many of the most delightful presents, which have obviously been made for babies or young children, are made from wood. Making things out of wood is even simpler nowadays with so many easy-to-use tools. And this is an area where fathers and grandfathers can happily be pressed into duty with the jigsaw. For instance, a wooden heart, decorated with a painted family tree could not be simpler. Naïve animal or soldier shapes are easy to draw and, as can be seen from the picture opposite, make delightful collections on the nursery shelf.

Sebastian
16.7.96

cross-stitch sampler

If you have never embroidered before, this is a good project to start with because cross stitch is truly easy. Remember that samplers were exactly that: samples of workers' stitching. Later they were used to teach the alphabet—and embroidery—to children. There are some delightfully quirky examples, where children have miscalculated the spacing of the alphabet. Sometimes letters are skipped altogether; sometimes (as here) they are repeated to balance things out. Imperfections are part of the charm. For this sampler, I have used part of an old linen tea towel rather than Aida cross-stitch fabric. This means that you have to use your eye and count more carefully than you would with the evenly woven Aida, but the result can be more characterful.

materials and equipment

14-in (35-cm) square of evenweave linen or Aida cloth

colored sewing thread and needle

small tapestry (scroll) frame

graph paper and colored pencils

embroidery needle (or have one needle for each color)

stranded embroidery thread

1 Divide the linen into quarters by folding it in half vertically, then horizontally. Using bright sewing thread, baste two guidelines across the creases, following the weave of the material. By keeping these lines straight, you can make sure the fabric does not become distorted.

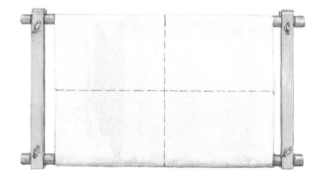

2 Mount the linen on a frame. Match the midpoints of the top and bottom edges of the fabric to the two lengths of webbing on the frame, then stitch the fabric to the webbing by hand. Slot the rollers onto the side struts and adjust them until the fabric is taut.

3 Draw the name and date you wish to include in your design on graph paper, as has been done on the example opposite. Depending on the length of the name your are working with, you may need to add extra symbols.

4 Each stitch is worked with three strands of embroidery thread over two threads of linen. For a smooth and even finish, the top stitch of each cross should lie in the same direction. Work each half of the cross with two actions to keep the stitches neat and regular.

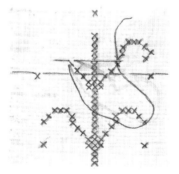

5 One square on the chart represents one cross stitch. Start stitching in the middle of the design and work outward, counting the stitches carefully. When the sampler is complete, remove it from the frame, unpick the guidelines, and press lightly from the back.

a nest of comforts

"It all looked so lovely that I almost thought a wizard must have been in there.
Mother said, yes, there had been a wizard around and that the wizard was Father,
and that he had conjured up a room for me that was to be my very own. This
was my birthday present, she said."

The Six Bullerby Children, Astrid Lindgren

The curtains across the bed in this little house **(left)** are made from an old patchwork quilt. Inside the walls are covered in pretty wrapping paper. The rag doll was found, headless, in a flea market; I spent a happy afternoon with her new owner making her a head and finding her some clothes to wear.

A voile curtain **(right)** with lots of pockets allows an ever-changing display of favorite treasures.

Now, at the age of six, the little girl who wakes up in this bedroom **(below)** can often be heard reading aloud the words embroidered on and around the clouds as she lies in bed.

a world—her own room—in a world —home—in a world …

something to wake up to

We can all remember lying awake in our childhood bedroom, slowly adjusting to the light of a new day, picking out once again the shapes and patterns discovered on the ceiling or in the wallpaper, seeking out the reassuring sight of our favorite pictures and familiar toys around us.

If you are preparing a nursery for a new child or moving an older child into a new bedroom, there are many ways in which to add a personal touch. Handcrafted and personalized quilts, pillows, window shades, and valances make a bedroom a warm, secure, and special environment for a child. Objects such as these make particularly lovely gifts because they gradually become part of a child's everyday visual landscape and are something they will remember forever.

Who knows what Lucca, the baby for whom the shade (left) was made, thought when she woke up in a her crib to find a family of pink patchwork elephants striding through a field of enormous flowers, with a little girl floating above them in a rose-patterned balloon. Admittedly, Lucca probably won't want marching pink elephants at her window when she is a teenager, but her handcrafted shade will still be an heirloom piece and will be much appreciated once she has children of her own.

In the tiny space seen on the page opposite, a mother with a background in theater design has created a magical bedroom for her two daughters. One sleeps up in the tree on a platform, while the younger daughter is cocooned in a little house complete with door and mail slot.

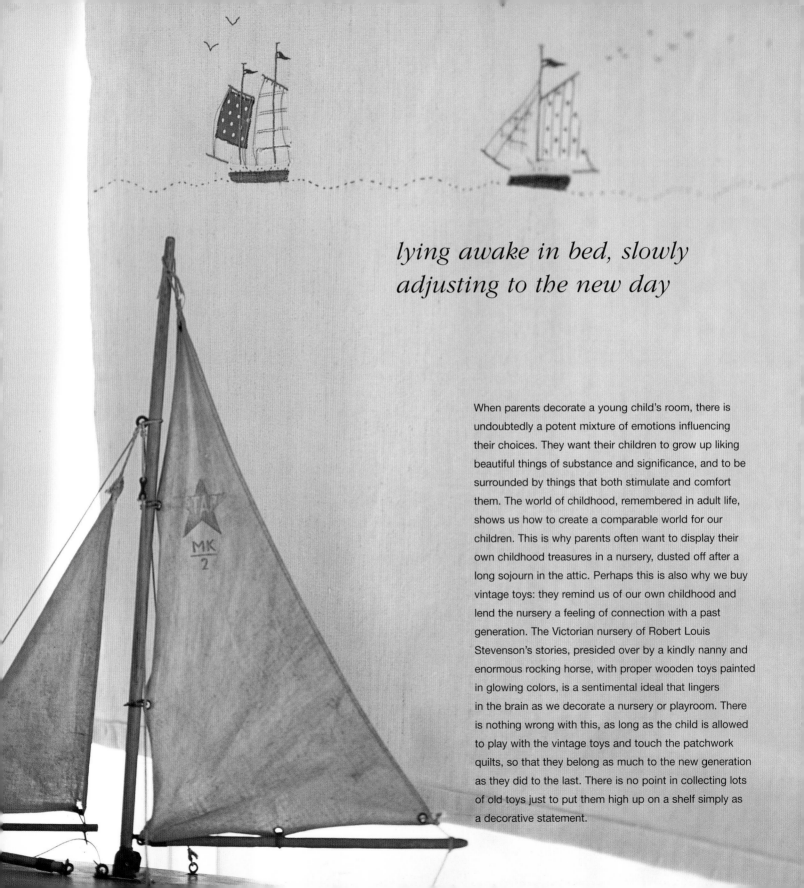

lying awake in bed, slowly adjusting to the new day

When parents decorate a young child's room, there is undoubtedly a potent mixture of emotions influencing their choices. They want their children to grow up liking beautiful things of substance and significance, and to be surrounded by things that both stimulate and comfort them. The world of childhood, remembered in adult life, shows us how to create a comparable world for our children. This is why parents often want to display their own childhood treasures in a nursery, dusted off after a long sojourn in the attic. Perhaps this is also why we buy vintage toys: they remind us of our own childhood and lend the nursery a feeling of connection with a past generation. The Victorian nursery of Robert Louis Stevenson's stories, presided over by a kindly nanny and enormous rocking horse, with proper wooden toys painted in glowing colors, is a sentimental ideal that lingers in the brain as we decorate a nursery or playroom. There is nothing wrong with this, as long as the child is allowed to play with the vintage toys and touch the patchwork quilts, so that they belong as much to the new generation as they did to the last. There is no point in collecting lots of old toys just to put them high up on a shelf simply as a decorative statement.

Vintage treasures make characterful curtains or shades. The map fabric **(right)** is far from being an antique, but the soft colors and slight wear, not to mention the bargain price, made it a find for a little boy's nursery. You can continue the theme with new, handcrafted decorative pieces that will be tomorrow's treasures. Later, these curtains will look wonderful in the bathroom or study of his adult home.

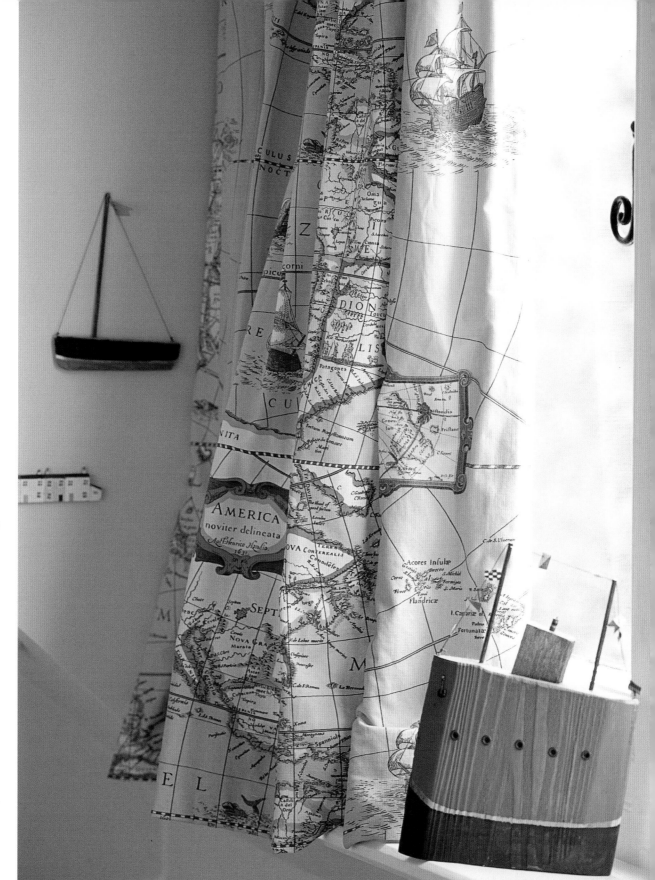

floral valance

This antique linen has been decorated with a scalloped edge and with stitched and appliquéd flowers to create a pretty window adornment. If you prefer, you could recycle an old runner or part of an embroidered tablecloth. The depth of the valance will depend very much on the proportions of your window, so make a paper template and pin it in place to be sure you have the correct size and shape.

materials and equipment

cardboard, paper, pencil, and ruler for template (see page 119)

linen

scraps of fabric for appliqué

embroidery thread and needle

²/₃-in (2-cm) wide velcro

lining fabric

²/₃-in (2-cm) wide strip of wood

staple gun

sewing kit

cutting out

A = window width

B = pelmet depth

from the linen:

1 strip measuring [A + 4 in (10 cm)] x [B + 2 in (5 cm)]

from lining fabric:

1 strip measuring [A + 1½ in (3 cm)] x B

velcro and strip of wood:

length = A

MAKING THE TEMPLATE

Measure the width of your window (A) and decide on the depth (B) of the valance. Decide how many scallops you want along the bottom: we cut 6, each 11-in (28-cm) wide, to fit a 66-in (168-cm) window. Divide A by your chosen number to find their width and draw the template (on page 119) to size. Trace it onto cardboard and cut it out.

Cut a long piece of paper to the finished size (A x B) and fold it in half. Position the template with side "b" along the fold and draw around the curve. Flip the template over, keeping the top edge aligned to the edge of the paper and draw along the curve again. Repeat to the end: you should end up with a half-scallop at each end.

1 Pin the template centrally to the linen so the scallops lie along the bottom edge. Cut along the curves, clipping down at a slight angle across the extra fabric at each end of the template.

2 Using tailor's chalk, draw a line 2 in (5 cm) from the curved edge of the linen as the baseline for the row of flowers. Create the floral design using a mixture of appliqué and embroidery. You will find all the necessary techniques described on pages 115–18. One flower template is provided on page 121.

3 Press, then unfold, a 2-in (5-cm) hem at each short end of the linen. Next attach the velcro to the right side of the valance (it will later be folded over to the back of the valance and sewn to the lining—see step 10.)

4 Separate the two parts of the velcro, then pin the looped side to right side of the linen, so it is 1 in (2 cm) down from the top edge and lies between the creases at each end. Baste, then machine stitch the velcro, working in the same direction along each side to avoid puckering.

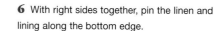

5 Now take the lining fabric. Press a hem under 1 in (2 cm) along the top edge and at each short edge. Unfold the side creases.

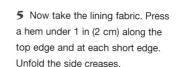

6 With right sides together, pin the linen and lining along the bottom edge.

7 Baste in place, just inside the scallops. Working with the linen uppermost and sewing between the creases on the lining, machine stitch ¼ in (6 mm) from the bottom edge, following the line of the curves exactly.

8 Trim away the excess lining fabric, following the edge of the linen. At the points where the curves meet, clip notches to within ⅛ in (3 mm) of the stitching so that the scallops will lie flat.

9 Turn right side out and carefully press the seam so that none of the lining is visible from the front. Refold and press the side creases.

10 Working from the right side and using a pressing cloth, press under the top corners of the linen (above the velcro) at a 45-degree angle. Fold the top edge again so that the velcro lies just below the fold, and press. Pin the lining in place covering the raw edges.

11 Baste and slipstitch the three unstitched sides of the lining to the linen.

12 Mount the strip of wood to the top of the window frame. Staple the remaining velcro to the wood. Press the two sides of velcro together to hang the valance.

every night I go afar into the Land of Nod …
and up the mountainsides of dreams

quilts & coverlets

There is something particularly lovely about making or giving a blanket or quilt for a newborn baby, whether it is a vintage find or a patchwork of simple knitted squares. All the quilts on this page are made from vintage fabrics, which are often softer and more durable than new ones: antique linen sheets have had their fibers softened by repeated washing and their colors bleached by drying in the hot sun for nearly a hundred years. Where fabric seems a little delicate, close quilting will strengthen it. I was thrilled to see the quilt that I made my niece

(shown here, above left) being used by her to cover her dolls. To me, this is much better than if it were wrapped in tissue paper and put away for safe keeping. If she uses it, she will remember it as something she played with in her childhood, which was, after all, the point of the gift. It is a good idea to look for damaged quilts at antique fairs. The damage is usually worse around the edge of the quilt, which means you can use the central piece to make a crib quilt or even a small single quilt for an older child.

On this quilt **(opposite, left)**, simple shapes inspired by folk art have been repeated using different antique textiles. The delicate machine applique is softened by close quilting, which not only creates a decorative surface texture, but also makes the quilt more durable.

A beloved toy elephant sits on a 1930s fan-pattern quilt **(opposite, right)**. Save your children's clothes and recycle them into an heirloom patchwork quilt or pillow.

Use simple embroidery to decorate crib sheets or pillowcases **(right)**, and turn them into treasures to hand down through the generations.

The primary colors of this baby blanket **(opposite and right)** make a refreshing change to the usual baby pinks and blues. No longer needed for a buggy, it now adorns the back of a chair in a family room, when it is not being pressed into service as a doll's bed cover.

Use an old blanket and scraps of fabric to create a comforting little blanket or play mat **(below)**. Perhaps embroider the child's name or a favorite line of children's poetry around the edge.

the most cherished object is one that has been handmade by a friend

The little baby blanket on this page (opposite and above) was made by a grandmother, a professional textile artist, for her first grandchild, and is an example of how the simplest idea can be used to create a work of art. Strips of the softest wool have been hand dyed with vegetable dyes to create washes of color through the fabric. Each little square has been pieced together with blanket stitch in contrasting colors. The little fabric hearts have been stitched on randomly, as though they had landed on the quilt of their own accord, like blessings.

Simple hand dyeing is actually quite easy to do, but if you cannot face it, look for vintage blankets and cut them into squares, dyeing each one a different color using machine dyes. Felt some of your old wool sweaters by putting them through a hot wash. If the sweaters are patterned, you can achieve some lovely effects by felting them. Felt is marvelous for appliqué because the edges do not fray. For instance, you could make the crib quilt project (see pages 36–39) from bright wool patches and felt appliqué, sewing the entire piece by hand.

*it's love that's been put into the object ...
that's more special to me than anything.*

There is something very comforting about brightly colored vintage blankets, the ends edged with broad satin ribbon and the label stitched properly into the corner. This is the sort of blanket that our mothers threw out with a first celebratory shake of the labor-saving duvet. A large, grown-up-size blanket is actually a rather nice present for a young child. Little ones can crawl around on them, picnic on them in the backyard, make tents out of them indoors on rainy days, take afternoon naps under them, and even take them to college to throw over an unsightly chair. When they are completely worn out, the blankets can be cut up to make something else or appliquéd with fabric to fashion a new blanket or large play cushion for a new child.

The log-cabin quilt, which—along with plenty of blankets—keeps the toys carried in this buggy **(above and opposite)** warm, was made by an eight-year-old girl and is now played with by her young daughters. This should be enough to give anyone the confidence to try their hand at log-cabin patchwork, which is very simple and grows quickly!

This handmade bear **(above left)** in his hand-knitted clothes is spoiled for choice when it comes to wonderful vintage blankets, their wool worn to a fine cozy softness. The new checked blanket he sits on is in the process of being transformed with simple motifs embroidered in wool.

crib quilt

What better way could there be to greet a new baby than with a patchwork crib quilt made especially for him or her? Not only is this an exquisite gift for any newborn, it is also guaranteed to become a treasured heirloom for generations to come. The quilt shown here was made from a selection of vintage fabrics, such as old linen sheeting, but new fabrics will work just as well—choose a nostalgic floral print in gentle, muted colors and team it with a soft cotton or linen for the plain blocks and the motifs. A selection of coordinated florals and patterned fabrics can also work well together.

materials and equipment

cardboard, ruler, and pencil for templates (see page 121)

plain fabric for the squares and the motifs (if you are using vintage fabrics, a variety of white linen scraps will create a soft look)

patterned fabrics for the squares

iron-on bonding web

embroidery thread and needle

soft flannel (for interlining the quilt)

backing fabric

edging fabric

plain linen for the top edging

sewing kit

1 The quilt pictured used 30 squares, each square measuring 4 x 4 in (10 cm x 10 cm). To calculate how many squares you will need, divide your desired width and length measurements by 4 if you are using inches, 10 if you are using metrics. To calculate the total number, multiply the number of squares that run across the quilt by the number that will run down the quilt.

2 Make a square template measuring 4¼ x 4¼ in (11 x 11 cm) from cardboard.

3 Assemble your plain and patterned fabric for the patchwork. Place the square template on the wrong side of the fabric, draw around it, and cut out the requisite number of plain and patterned squares. Position your template carefully to enable you to get as many squares as possible from each piece of material.

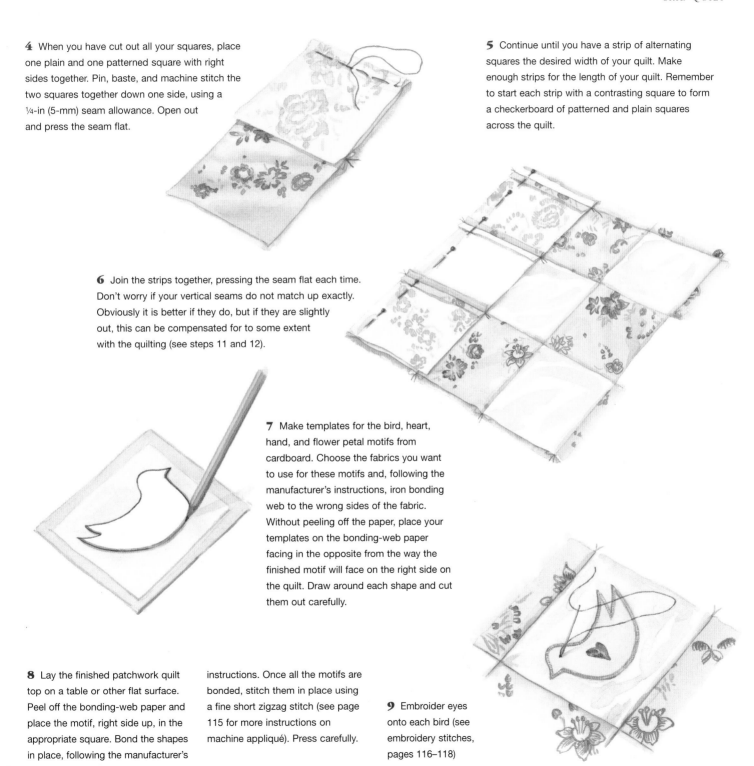

4 When you have cut out all your squares, place one plain and one patterned square with right sides together. Pin, baste, and machine stitch the two squares together down one side, using a ¼-in (5-mm) seam allowance. Open out and press the seam flat.

5 Continue until you have a strip of alternating squares the desired width of your quilt. Make enough strips for the length of your quilt. Remember to start each strip with a contrasting square to form a checkerboard of patterned and plain squares across the quilt.

6 Join the strips together, pressing the seam flat each time. Don't worry if your vertical seams do not match up exactly. Obviously it is better if they do, but if they are slightly out, this can be compensated for to some extent with the quilting (see steps 11 and 12).

7 Make templates for the bird, heart, hand, and flower petal motifs from cardboard. Choose the fabrics you want to use for these motifs and, following the manufacturer's instructions, iron bonding web to the wrong sides of the fabric. Without peeling off the paper, place your templates on the bonding-web paper facing in the opposite from the way the finished motif will face on the right side on the quilt. Draw around each shape and cut them out carefully.

8 Lay the finished patchwork quilt top on a table or other flat surface. Peel off the bonding-web paper and place the motif, right side up, in the appropriate square. Bond the shapes in place, following the manufacturer's instructions. Once all the motifs are bonded, stitch them in place using a fine short zigzag stitch (see page 115 for more instructions on machine appliqué). Press carefully.

9 Embroider eyes onto each bird (see embroidery stitches, pages 116–118)

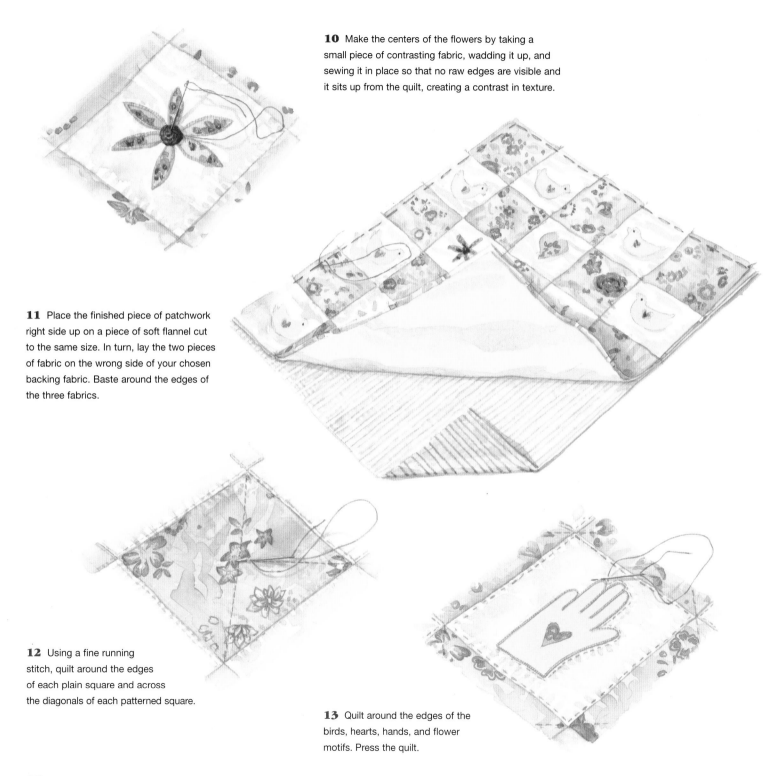

10 Make the centers of the flowers by taking a small piece of contrasting fabric, wadding it up, and sewing it in place so that no raw edges are visible and it sits up from the quilt, creating a contrast in texture.

11 Place the finished piece of patchwork right side up on a piece of soft flannel cut to the same size. In turn, lay the two pieces of fabric on the wrong side of your chosen backing fabric. Baste around the edges of the three fabrics.

12 Using a fine running stitch, quilt around the edges of each plain square and across the diagonals of each patterned square.

13 Quilt around the edges of the birds, hearts, hands, and flower motifs. Press the quilt.

14 Cut 3 strips of binding fabric 1½ in (3 cm) wide and the same length as the two sides and the bottom of the quilt. Starting with the bottom edge of the quilt, place the binding right side down on top of the quilt and stitch ⅓ in (1 cm) in from the raw edges. Press.

15 Trim the seam, then turn the binding over to the back of the quilt. Fold the raw edge under and neatly slipstitch it to the back of the quilt. Repeat with both the side edges.

16 To finish the top, cut a strip of linen 4 in (10 cm) deep and the width of the quilt. Press the strip in half lengthwise. Use the technique described in steps 7 and 8 to appliqué heart and star motifs to one half of the folded strip. You could embroider the child's name around the heart.

17 With right sides together and raw edges aligned, pin, baste, and machine the long appliquéd side of the top binding to the top of the quilt. Trim the seam.

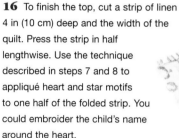

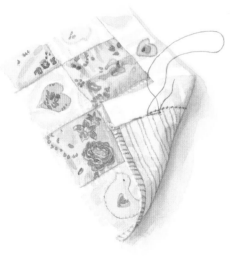

18 Fold over the top binding piece, press under a hem, and slipstitch the back edge to the back of the quilt. At the sides, turn the raw edges under and slipstitch together. Press the quilt.

the homes we make make us homey

cozy corners

In *Little Women,* Jo is always retreating to her garret with a bag of apples to read her books under a comforter on an old sofa. It is her cozy place. Children need their own cozy spot, even if it is the corner of a family room, where they can curl up with their books and read, either on the floor or in a comfy chair. Cushions and pillows definitely make hard surfaces feel more inviting. My husband still has the enormous patchwork floor cushion his mother made for him when he was a little boy. Make each child a special cushion to snuggle up to. There are so many different ways in which you can personalize a cushion: spend an afternoon with some plain fabric and

Both reader and listener need to be comfortably settled when it comes to storytime. Pile pillows onto beds and choose a corner of a family room to make into a cozy place for reading or being read to. Vintage eiderdowns have an instantly softening effect, while damaged quilts can be given a new lease of life as cushions.

41

Use scraps and remnants of fabric to make colorful pillowcovers to cheer and soften the corners of a child's room. A sunny corner of a playroom **(opposite)** has been made very cozy by having an armchair covered with a cheerful quilt. Surrounded by all the familiar members of the nursery, a child just discovering the pleasure of a good read could snuggle down very comfortably.

my whole life is in that quilt … all my joys and sorrows are stitched into those little pieces

fabric paint, decorating the fabric with your child. Use the appliqué techniques described in this book (see page 115) to create a scene from one of their favorite books.

We wince slightly at the cloths embroidered by the thousand in the 1930s and 1940s depicting girls in dainty bonnets and crinolines gathering flowers under elaborate rose arbors. However, a nest of pillows made from these is a delight to a little girl. Add to this an extra snuggly cushion or huge squashy beanbag made from old blankets. Keep a lovely old eiderdown or quilt on the side of the couch, so there is something warm and familiar to wrap up in while reading or watching television.

log-cabin pillow

Next time you find a traycloth depicting a crinoline-skirted lady, why not turn it into a pillowcover for a little girl's room? You could also use a scene from fabric that you have used elsewhere in her room, perhaps for curtains, surrounded with a coordinating check or ticking. Pillows are great presents for a new baby—they liven up the nursery and are comfy for Mom during nighttime feeds. This pillow features two rows of log-cabin, but you could just do one if you prefer. If you are experienced at sewing, make the back in two overlapping pieces and embroider button covers, like those on page 53, for a special touch.

materials and equipment

embroidered or picture patch measuring 9 x 7 in (22 x 17 cm)

plain linen

contrasting fabric

stranded embroidery thread

pillow form

sewing kit

cutting out

from plain linen:

2 pieces (A & B) measuring 11 x 3 in (27 x 8 cm)

2 pieces (C & D) measuring 9 x 3 in (22 x 8 cm)

from contrasting fabric:

2 pieces (E & F) measuring 17 x 5½ in (40.5 x 14 cm)

2 pieces (G & H) measuring 38 x 11.5 cm (16 x 5 in)

for the back of the pillow:

1 piece of fabric to 21 x 21 in (50 x 50 cm)

seam allowances of ½ in (1.5 cm) included

1 With right sides together, pin a long edge of strip A to the top of the decorated patch, with the left-hand edges aligned. Baste and machine stitch to 1½ in (3 cm) from the edge of the patch. Fingertip press the seam away from the patch.

2 Working counterclockwise around the patch, pin, baste, and sew strip C right sides together to the top left-hand corner of strip A and down the left-hand side of the patch. Fingertop press the seam away from patch.

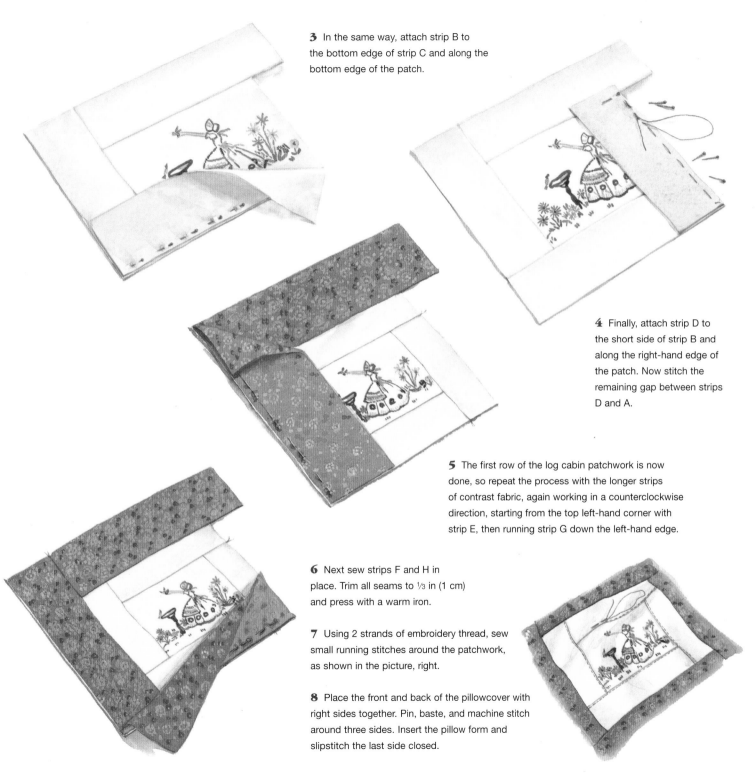

3 In the same way, attach strip B to the bottom edge of strip C and along the bottom edge of the patch.

4 Finally, attach strip D to the short side of strip B and along the right-hand edge of the patch. Now stitch the remaining gap between strips D and A.

5 The first row of the log cabin patchwork is now done, so repeat the process with the longer strips of contrast fabric, again working in a counterclockwise direction, starting from the top left-hand corner with strip E, then running strip G down the left-hand edge.

6 Next sew strips F and H in place. Trim all seams to ⅓ in (1 cm) and press with a warm iron.

7 Using 2 strands of embroidery thread, sew small running stitches around the patchwork, as shown in the picture, right.

8 Place the front and back of the pillowcover with right sides together. Pin, baste, and machine stitch around three sides. Insert the pillow form and slipstitch the last side closed.

45

This tabletop **(opposite and far left)** has been painted to resemble a stretch of fields by the sea, where a child can use his imagination and a few toy animals for hours of play.

Here **(near left)** a small but perfectly proportioned child's desk, made in Paris early in the twentieth century, is teamed with the ideal-sized chair. The chair cushion has been made from remnants of Victorian patchwork.

a patchwork of fields painted on a tabletop
creates a world within a world for hours of play

tables & chairs

Children love to have their own little chair and somewhere to write and draw, preferably in the kitchen or family room, with perhaps an extra chair for small guests.

Antique malls abound with children's chairs and tables. Some are extremely valuable, in oak or elm. Many are less expensive, and perhaps a little more worn, but can be cleaned up or repainted to make an unusual and practical gift for a child. Many of them are attractive enough to decorate a room long after the child has outgrown them, waiting for new occupants in the next generation.

Of course, the chairs and tables do not have to be old. The inexpensive set of table and chairs shown on the page opposite is brand-new, and has been transformed by paint and fabric into a unique gift for a child. The table would be a lovely project for older siblings to make for a new baby in the family. The scenery can be changed from time to time: you could spend an afternoon together recreating a setting from a favorite book, or help your child to understand the geography of where he lives and how he can walk to school by painting a map on the table.

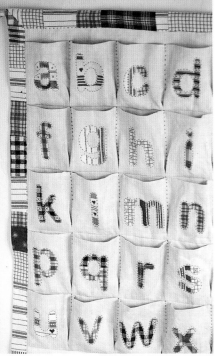

alphabet sorter

Children seem to amass a huge collection of tiny objects that have a habit of multiplying secretly under tables and chairs all over the house. Hair ornaments, plastic alphabet letters, lego, innumerable party-bag presents, odd socks … all of these can be stored in the pockets of this door or wall hanging. We have used the letters of the alphabet for decoration, but you could use animals, flowers, or whatever you like instead. If you do choose to use an alphabet, a good way to create templates is to pick a favorite font from your computer and print out suitably sized letters.

materials and equipment

39 x 60 in (100 x 150 cm) plain linen (I used an antique sheet)

scraps and remnants of striped and checked fabrics in reds and blues

paper and pen for templates

iron-on bonding web

red and blue stranded embroidery thread

2 large cup hooks

28-in (70-cm) length of ⅔-in (2-cm) diameter wooden doweling, painted white

sewing kit

cutting out

from the white linen:

1 rectangle measuring 24 x 31 in (60 x 80 cm) for the main panel

5 strips measuring 8 x 25 in (20 x 63 cm) for the pockets

1 strip measuring 3 x 21 in (6 x 50 cm) for the casing

1 Finish each end of the casing with a ½-in (1.5-cm) double hem and press under ½ in (1.5 cm) along the long edges. With the right side up, pin and baste the strip centrally to the back of the main panel ⅔ in (2 cm) from the top edge. Machine stitch close to each long edge.

2 To make the patchwork borders, cut a selection of pieces from the fabric scraps 2½ in (7 cm) square. Leaving a narrow seam allowance, machine stitch together to form four strips, two 24 in (60 cm) long and two 31 in (80 cm) long.

3 Press all the seams on the border strips open, then press under a ½-in (1.5-cm) hem along one long side of each strip.

4 Create the letter templates by printing the alphabet from a computer or draw them free style. The largest should be 3 in (8 cm) high, except Z which is just 1½ in (3 cm) so it can fit next to Y. Trace each letter onto the paper side of bonding web, reversing the shapes. Cut them out roughly, peel off the paper backing, and iron them to the wrong side of the patterned fabric scraps. Cut out carefully around the pencil outlines.

5 Neaten the top edge of each pocket strip with a zigzag or overlocking stitch, then press under a 5-cm (2-in) fold.

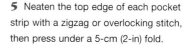

6 Using tailor's chalk, mark the folding points along the bottom of each pocket strip. Leave a ½-in (1.5-cm) seam allowance at each end, then mark five 4-in (10-cm) pockets with a 1-in (2.5-cm) gap between each one. Mark the center of each small space: these will become the box pleats that give fullness to the pockets. Mark the corresponding points along the top edge and unfold the hem. Repeat on each pocket strip.

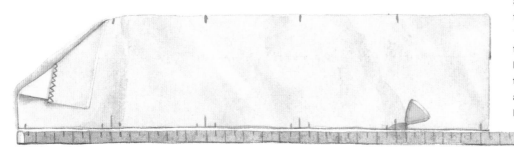

7 Keeping them in alphabetical order, iron a letter centrally onto each pocket space (except for the Y, and Z, which both go on the final pocket). Thread the machine with cream thread and work a round of narrow zigzag stitch over the raw edges of the letters. Embellish the letters with a little hand stitching, using a single strand of embroidery thread, then work a line of running stitch around each one to define the shape.

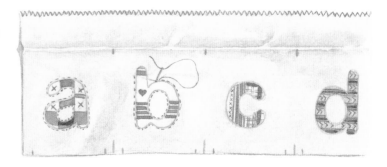

8 Press the top fold back in position along the first strip. With right sides together and working along the lower edge, match the sides of the four pleats and pin them in place. Baste and machine stitch for 2 in (5 cm) to divide the pockets. Repeat for the other pocket strips.

9 Open the pleats and pin each seam line to the center point behind it. Line up the folds with the marks along the top edge and press to create the box pleats. Baste and machine stitch them in place, ¼ in (6 mm) from the bottom edge. Do the same on the other strips.

10 With the right side up, lay the first pocket strip (A–E) in position centrally along the top of the main panel so the top edge of the pocket lies 3 in (8 cm) below the raw edge of the main panel. Turn the pocket strip back so the right side faces down. Pin, baste, and machine stitch across the pleats, making a seam allowance of ½ in (1.5 cm). Turn the pocket strip back up and press along the fold. Baste each end of the strip to the main panel.

11 Join the other four pocket strips in the same way (in alphabetical order), making sure that when they are stitched in place, each one butts up neatly to the bottom of the strip above.

12 Pin the center of each pleat to the main fabric to separate the pockets, then sew them securely in place with a line of running stitch worked with a double length of embroidery thread.

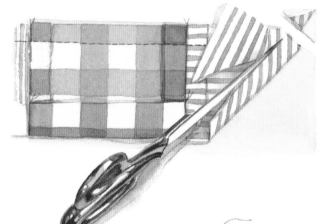

13 Place the main panel face down on a flat surface. Take the first short patchwork border strip and, with the right side down and raw edges aligned, pin and baste it to the top of the panel. Machine stitch just above the casing, starting and finishing ½ in (1.5 cm) from each side edge and making a seam allowance of ½ in (1.5 cm).

14 Fold up the two corners of the patchwork strip at 45 degrees so the raw edges meet. Press in place. Trim the excess fabric to leave a seam allowance of ¼ in (6 mm), and clip the corners.

15 Turn the border strip to the right side and press the fold. Secure the folded edge to the main panel with a line of running stitch. Join the other three border strips the same way, concealing the raw edges of the pocket strips with the two long strips.

16 Slipstitch together the two folds at each corner to form a miter.

17 Screw the cup hooks firmly into the wall, slide the length of dowelling through the casing at the back of the sorter, and hang.

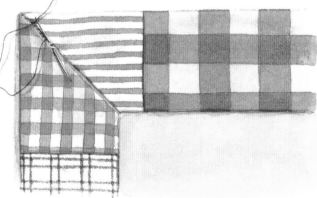

Look for vintage tea towels and tablecloths with embroidery in pretty colors around the corners: these are most useful for converting into dresses. Buttons, too, are a very good way of livening up readymade children's clothes. Make a few hand-embroidered covered buttons to sew onto a niece's dress or a nephew's romper suit. They would be a lovely present to mail since they are small and light.

new clothes from old

Modern technology and the employment by Western designers of inexpensive foreign labor have led us to take intricate embroidery for granted. Now, when we unwrap parcels of clothes from the attic or come across racks of them in antique stores, we marvel at how our mothers and grandmothers ever had the time or patience to fashion the little hand-smocked dresses in soft striped or checked cotton that bring to mind summer days in the gardens of our childhood.

Old tablecloths, napkins sheets, and embroidered cloths stashed away in our grandmother's drawers are all fantastic raw materials for little girls' dresses. Secondhand stores are a source of old linen sheets from which to make a simple dress, using vintage embroidery for the collars and cuffs. The dress on the opposite page was made from an old sheet and two corners of a vintage tablecloth. If you do not sew at all, buy a plain white dress and appliqué single flower patches somewhere quirky, or add covered buttons. You can also dye cotton and linen: mix up packs of machine dye—try red and pink, or blue and gray. Some of the best effects are achieved with repeated dyeings using slight variations in the amount of dye or even different colors.

There is no mystery about simple embroidery: even a row of cross stitch or simple running stitch add charm to children's clothing. Anyone can draw a simple little flower with needle and thread. The little hand-knitted cardigan here was a flea-market find that has been decorated with embroidery in wool for a baby doll. The gingham dress, seen opposite, was one of two made from an enormous nineteenth-century French homespun petticoat, perhaps made for Sunday best as it had a ruffle and cotton lace trim. This gave a ready-hemmed skirt, while the dress cuff and collars were made from an old linen sheet and

Tiny knitted dolls' clothes are unbearably touching. Here, two little cardigans **(this page)**, probably knitted for a dress-up doll in the 1960s, have been rescued from a trash bag in a flea market, washed, and embroidered, to be turned into rather special presents for a little girl who is crazy about her Barbie.

54

The repair under the sleeve of this little dress **(above and right)** made from an old French petticoat has been done with a similar nineteenth-century homespun fabric, and is a deliberate imitation of the charming and embellishing repairs you see on old peasant clothing.

A row of appealing vintage children's dresses hangs in a pretty painted armoire in a decorative antique store. The fabrics are all softened in texture and color by years of use, but they are so carefully handsewn that even today they could be worn.

The addition of intricate smocking and embroidery to simple striped cotton fabric conjures up an image of the sea, and of a small girl racing about on a beach in the height of a 1950's summer. The red smock was probably the Sunday-best attire of a French child toward the end of the nineteenth century. Even the way the buttons are sewn on contributes to the overall design.

embroidered by hand. The result is a unique dress that is easy to wear and wash. There is something rather appealing about a petticoat worn by someone a century ago being transformed into a dress for an active twenty-first-century six-year-old. Antique clothing can be found very cheaply, especially in France. What children used to wear as undergarments can be made, with the simplest of alterations, into the most delightful summer clothing for today's child.

Some people do not like the idea of dressing their children in secondhand or vintage clothes. I love to think about the people who made these clothes, and find the tiny embellishments and carefully sewn-on buttons extremely touching. Certainly I couldn't help a stab of sadness that something as precious as the hand-smocked and embroidered dresses seen on these pages had found their way into a flea market. However, it seemed that the best tribute to the hands that made them with such love would be to give them as presents to small children, to start their lives afresh as heirlooms in a different family. Alternatively, create your own heirloom, even if it is just by adding beautiful mother-of-pearl buttons sewn on with contrasting thread, a little row of red cross stitches around a cuff or along a seam, or hand-embroidered daisies around the neckline of a readymade white cotton dress.

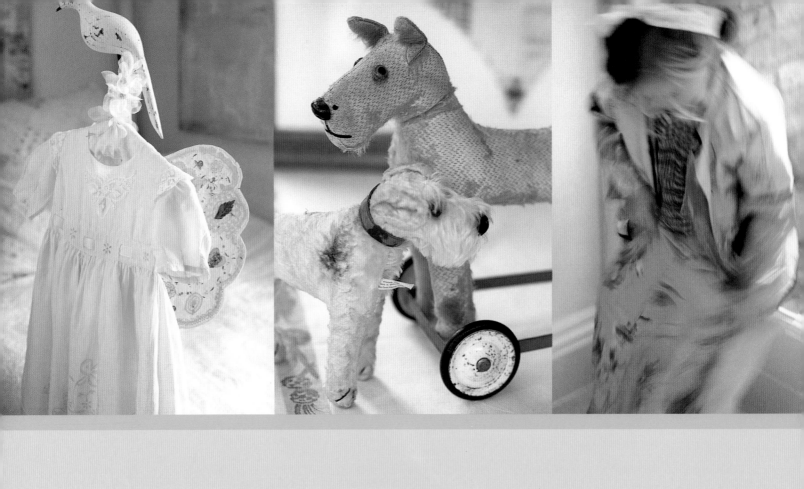

toys & playthings

"When I am grown to man's estate

I shall be very proud and great,

And tell the other girls and boys

Not to meddle with my toys."

A Child's Garden of Verses, Robert Louis Stevenson

dolls have lives, too: *they socialize*

Dolls are often our very first friends. We share our secrets with them and spend hours dressing and undressing them, changing and rearranging their hairstyles, setting them in a social milieu of our own making, and putting them to bed.

It is fascinating to watch a small child busy at play with her dolls. Each dolly in the nursery has a name and identity of her own, and many children become very involved in the fantasy lives of their dolls. Dolls do not have to be expensive. It is impossible to predict what will appeal to a child. Sometimes the most glamorous all-talking, all-crying doll with retractable hair and tear-spurting eyes will be rebuffed in favor of the simplest rag doll with a stitched smile and crinkled yarn hair. Nearly all of the dolls on these pages were found in secondhand stores, re-clothed, and sent to the loving care of my youngest niece.

For the very best tea parties, make sure that all dolls are suitably attired. Plan the seating arrangement carefully and create pretty table settings by using old handkerchiefs for cloths and tiny scraps of linen rolled up and secured with an artificial flower. Make real sandwiches and cut them up using a miniature cookie cutter, or cut up an adult cake into doll-sized portions and sprinkle with powdered sugar.

Playing with dolls is part of a child's introduction to socializing, and a lot of social skills can be acquired in the planning and execution of an elaborate dolls' tea party. For instance, it is important to make sure all the dolls have somewhere to sit, and that there is enough tea and cake to go around. It is never too early to introduce your child to the art of stylish entertaining!

Fill eggcups with glossy red berries for a strawberry tea or with small colored candy. Spend a little time in the yard collecting tiny flowers for the tea table. An afternoon spent attending to miniature things reminds us what it is like to be very small.

... *look beautiful*

Barbie. The word sends shivers of political correctness down the spines of women who were among the first and most fixated of Barbie owners. When looking for Barbies to use in this book, I was slightly surprised to discover that a friend still has her childhood Barbie and makes her a new outfit for her annual vacation!

Dressing a doll is often the first opportunity we have to express our developing taste in clothes. Watching my aunt as she conjured up a

fashionable cape out of elegant blue tweed lined with red satin for my Barbie was a heart-stopping moment in my seventh year. Dolls' clothes are very good presents to send by mail. In the black-and-white films of my childhood, the heroine's dresses were always delivered in glamorous boxes tied up with satin ribbon and were lifted out of tissue paper with an enticing rustle. Imagine the pleasure such a delivery would bring to a Barbie-obsessed child.

Holding a Barbie for the first time in years as we photographed these pages, I confess I took exactly the same amount of pleasure in winding her silky tresses into a chignon as I had when I was six years old. It was utterly thrilling to design and make her clothes, in particular the dress (**opposite**), a bit like the one Audrey Hepburn wears in *Sabrina Fair*, with layers of the finest organza wafting about her minute waist. It was even more exciting to watch the expression on a small girl's face when she first unwrapped this new outfit for her favorite doll from a small, beautifully presented box.

... and sleep

Putting dolly to bed can be a very good way of introducing the unpopular idea of bedtime! I once spent over an hour happily indulging a four-year-old girl as she went about the serious business of changing no fewer than six dolls into their various arrays of nightwear and carefully tucking them into their individual little beds before she would even contemplate allowing me to do the same for her.

Look around any collectibles market, and you may find a good selection of old dolls' beds, nearly all of them made by amateurs. Often they still have their original paint, which can be an inspiring starting point for a handmade quilt and bedlinen. These hand-painted cradles and cribs are quite valuable now, and make lovely christening presents for a little girl, adding an authentic decorative touch to a nursery. Make a little mattress, using batting, and tiny pillows. Embroider a line from

The little doll so cozily tucked in here **(above left)** is sleeping under an old baby blanket and a beautifully embroidered tray cloth.

Use pretty faded florals **(above and opposite)** or old nursery fabrics to make pillows and quilts for dolls' beds. Decorate them with embroidered words for the lucky "poupée" who will be sleeping in the bed!

a lullaby across the top of a sheet, or "sweet dreams" across the pillow. If you don't like sewing or don't have time, look for small pieces of blanket and cloths with an attractive edging. Alternatively, use some of the fabric you have used to decorate the girl in question's bedroom. It is a charming idea to use some of the bedlinen she had as a baby, perhaps her favorite little baby blanket or her first shawl. This way, she continues to have around her the things that mean most to her as she grows away from babyhood.

The wicker basket on this page was lined as a present for a little girl who had just acquired a baby brother. Her mother felt that a new doll and pretty basket would encourage her daughter to imitate her mother as she looked after her new baby, and lessen the feelings of jealousy and exclusion that often accompany the birth of a sibling. Some doll's beds are so beautiful that they can remain on display long after a child has ceased to play with dolls. The Victorian wirework bed on this page, bought by a grandmother as a christening present for her new granddaughter, is an example. The bedding and miniature quilt were made from antique and vintage textiles. In years to come, the whole ensemble will become a valuable heirloom.

Every need of the dolls in this nursery **(opposite)** has been catered for—a rocking swan to play on, a pretty crib with bedlinen made from vintage fabric, and hand-knitted blankets. A small set of drawers has been painted and lined to use as a clothes chest, and the gentle confusion of soft colors creates a charming atmosphere for a child's play area.

Antique stores and malls often have delightful handmade wooden cribs, wicker baskets, or even tiny wirework beds **(this page)**, which can be dressed up with vintage fabrics.

This quirky collection of much-loved hand-knitted toys **(opposite)** was made by a family friend for four children over many Christmases and birthdays.

Colorful felt clothes are simple to make and lend a rakish air to this rogues' gallery **(above)**. One of these toys inspired the project overleaf.

stuffed toys

Stuffed toys have been made as presents for young children for centuries, using whatever scraps of homespun fabric and yarn were on hand in the piece bag. With floppity ears, sagging tummies, and button eyes, they are the most characterful and endearing members of the nursery set. Little rag dolls and soft toys with simple shapes are very easy to make. If you are lucky enough to be able to knit, there are many patterns for appealing toys. Knit a bear and then make simple clothes from colorful felt so a child can have the fun of dressing the

toy in different outfits—if you use felt, there is no need to hem edges. The important thing is to keep the shapes simple and to find the right raw materials: scraps of old baby blankets, bright felts, and shiny tortoiseshell buttons all help lend character to your creation.

You can find ancient and battered nursery veterans in all sorts of places, from flea markets to antique fairs, where the prices they fetch may raise an eyebrow. Even so, the quiet dignity of a once-loved bear as he ponders his fate among the bricabrac is hard to resist.

mister rabbit

This is probably the most complicated project in this book, and requires very precise cutting and stitching. Anyone with dressmaking skills will be able to do it, but if you are a beginner, it might be better to start with some of the other projects. The main thing is to exercise great care when stuffing the head and body to achieve a nice shape. You do not have to use fur for the head: a soft felt or piece of blanket would also work, although the fur contrasts nicely with the felt clothes.

materials and equipment

pencil and paper for templates (see page 120)

gray fake fur or mohair for head, ears, paws, and tail

muslin for body, arms, ears, and tail

polyester toy stuffing

scraps of black and orange felt

black stranded embroidery thread

5 small buttons

green felt for vest

blue felt for jodhpurs

red felt for coat and boots

checked ribbon or strip of fabric

sewing kit

cutting out

See page 120 for templates. Use a photocopier to enlarge these by approximately 200 per cent. The fur pieces should be cut with the pile running down, following the direction of the arrow. The muslin has the grain running from top to bottom. Clip notches into the seam allowance where indicated by small triangles.

from the fur:

2 paws

2 heads (one reversed)

1 gusset

2 ears

1 tail

from the muslin:

2 arms

2 bodies

2 ears

1 tail

from the green felt:

1 front and 1 back vest

from the blue felt:

2 jodhpur pieces

from the red felt:

4 boots

2 soles

I jacket (along fold)

2 sleeves

1 pocket

from the orange felt:

2 outer eyes

from the black felt:

2 inner eyes

The seam allowance is ¼ in (6 mm), unless directed. All the seams should be pinned and basted before being stitched by machine or by hand.

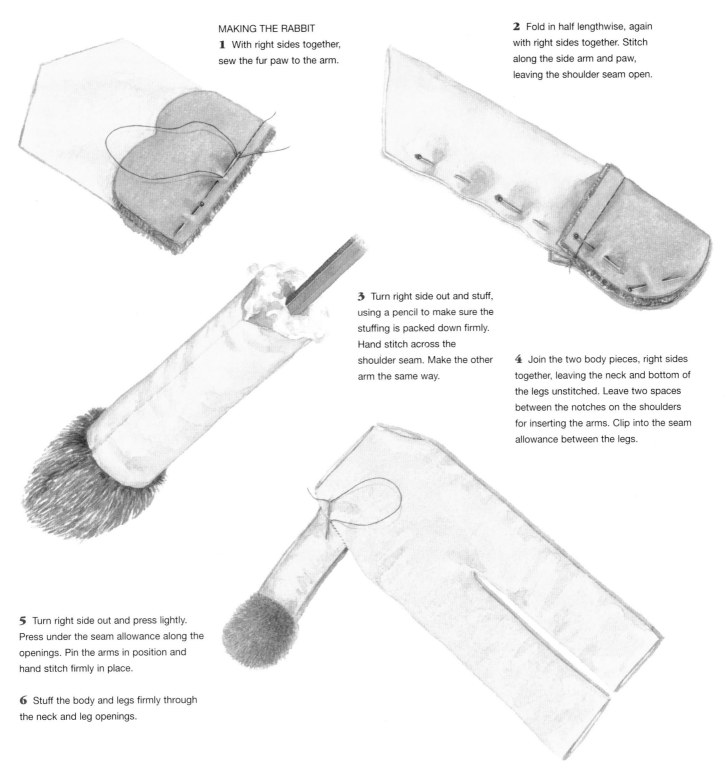

MAKING THE RABBIT

1 With right sides together, sew the fur paw to the arm.

2 Fold in half lengthwise, again with right sides together. Stitch along the side arm and paw, leaving the shoulder seam open.

3 Turn right side out and stuff, using a pencil to make sure the stuffing is packed down firmly. Hand stitch across the shoulder seam. Make the other arm the same way.

4 Join the two body pieces, right sides together, leaving the neck and bottom of the legs unstitched. Leave two spaces between the notches on the shoulders for inserting the arms. Clip into the seam allowance between the legs.

5 Turn right side out and press lightly. Press under the seam allowance along the openings. Pin the arms in position and hand stitch firmly in place.

6 Stuff the body and legs firmly through the neck and leg openings.

7 Fold and stitch the pleat on each head piece. With right sides together, stitch one side of the gusset between the notches on the first head piece. Join the second head piece to the other side of the gusset, leaving the neck open. Turn right side out.

8 Sew the felt eyes in place, using the pattern piece as a position guide. Using a double thickness of six-stranded embroidery thread, sew four straight stitches for the nose and mouth.

9 With right sides together, join a muslin and a fur ear, leaving the bottom edge unstitched. Turn right side out, then fold the seam allowance to the inside. Do the same with the other ear.

10 Fold both corners of the fur side to meet at the front and stitch in place across the bottom edge. Hand stitch the ears onto the head across the pleat line. To give the rabbit his quirky look, they face in opposite directions.

11 Stuff the head tightly and hand stitch it to the body around the neck edge, lining up the front and back seams with the notches.

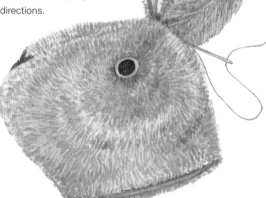

MAKING THE CLOTHES

12 Sew the buttons in a straight line down the front of the vest. Join the side and shoulder seams of the front and back along one side only, with right sides together. Turn right side out, put the vest on the rabbit, and hand stitch the other two seams.

13 Join the side and inside leg seams of the jodhpur pieces. Clip into the seam allowance between the legs. Mark the pleat lines with pins, then baste and machine stitch them in place. Turn right side out and hand stitch the jodhpurs to the rabbit's body around the waist.

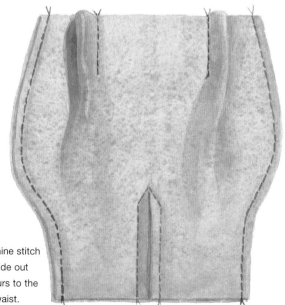

14 Stitch the side seams of the two boots and turn out. Matching the front and back notches to the seam lines, sew the soles in place with wrong sides together, so the seam allowance is on the right side. Trim the surplus fabric close to the stitching. Using six strands of black embroidery thread, make six parallel straight stitches for the laces and tie the ends of the thread into a bow.

15 Stuff the boots firmly to create the feet, then slip the rabbit's legs into the top of the boots, up to the boot lines marked on the jodhpur pattern. Hand stitch the top edges securely through both the jodhpurs and the body.

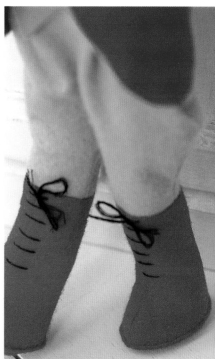

16 The seam allowance on the jacket is ⅛ in (3 mm). With wrong sides together, stitch the collar seams. Turn the jacket the other way out and, with right sides together, stitch the shoulder seams.

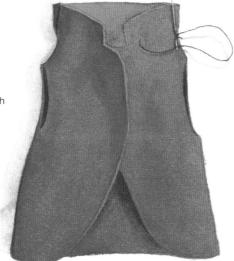

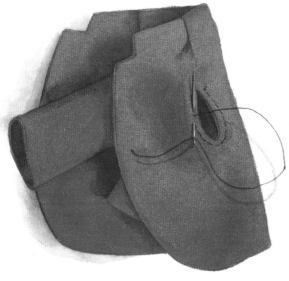

17 Join the two sides of each sleeve. With right sides together and the notches lined up with the shoulder seams, sew the sleeves into the armholes. Turn right side out and sew the pocket on the right-hand side of the jacket. Tie the checked ribbon or fabric around the rabbit's neck for a cravat.

18 Finally, sew the felt and fur tail pieces together with right sides together, leaving the top edge open. Turn right side out and fold under the seam allowance along the top edge. Slipstitch the tail to the rabbit just below the waistline, so the top edge is concealed by the hem of the jacket.

73

painted wooden toys

Toys have been made out of wood in more or less the same shapes and forms for hundreds of years. Horses, soldiers, dolls' houses and beds, pull-along animals, arks full of tiny carved and painted animals have long been whittled or carved with varying degrees of skill. Antique and vintage toys are extremely popular with collectors, and the price they fetch would probably astonish their makers.

The appeal of vintage wooden toys is in the simple, strong shapes and the way paint has faded and worn into the grain of the wood through years of having been played with. Another reason these toys have such personality is that they were, on the whole, made for a particular child. The toymaker thought of and was inspired by the love for the child as he worked, which cannot help but add some indefinable spark of magic to the finished toy. I am reminded of Miss Jenny Wren, the doll's dressmaker in Dickens' *Our Mutual Friend*, who works in the dreary grime of London's East End, a neighborhood that is "anything but" flowery, and yet as she works, she smells

Model farms for children to play with can be elaborate indoor affairs, like the one on these pages which was probably made for a child by an enthusiastic amateur carpenter. With today's labor-saving tools, a farm like this would be relatively easy to replicate. The same skills could be employed to make forts, dolls' houses, or a multi-story garage for model cars.

"miles of flowers. I smell roses, till I think I see the rose-leaves lying in heaps, bushels, on the floor … I smell the white and the pink May in the hedges, and all sorts of flowers that I never was among."

Some wooden toys, such as the ocean liner and the little rabbit in the pictures above, really are very simple to make. The ocean liner is particularly inventive: not only does it float, it is a covetable decorative piece for any stage of a person's life, and would therefore be a very unusual present to make for a child. You can achieve a more authentic, rustic look by sanding off hard edges; then raise the grain of the wood before painting it by running a blowtorch lightly over the surface, followed by scrubbing the wood with a wire brush in the direction of the grain. This also has the effect of darkening new wood, which is always a better base for the weathered paint effect described on page 114.

o it's I that am the captain of a tidy little ship,
of a ship that goes a-sailing on the pond

The toymaker is a magical figure in children's literature, from Gepetto, the creator of *Pinocchio*, to the friendly toymaker in *Chitty Chitty Bang Bang*. Tell a young child that a toy has been made by hand, and he may believe that it is imbued with special powers, a toy of "fairy land, Where all the children dine at five, And all the playthings come alive." Certainly, it would not be hard for a child to imagine this exquisitely whittled and carved toy acrobat and horse **(right)**, a family treasure handed down through two generations, whirling around the nursery shelf after dark. Hand-painted wooden toys such as those seen on these pages are often sufficiently stylish and interesting to be displayed and played with in a family room.

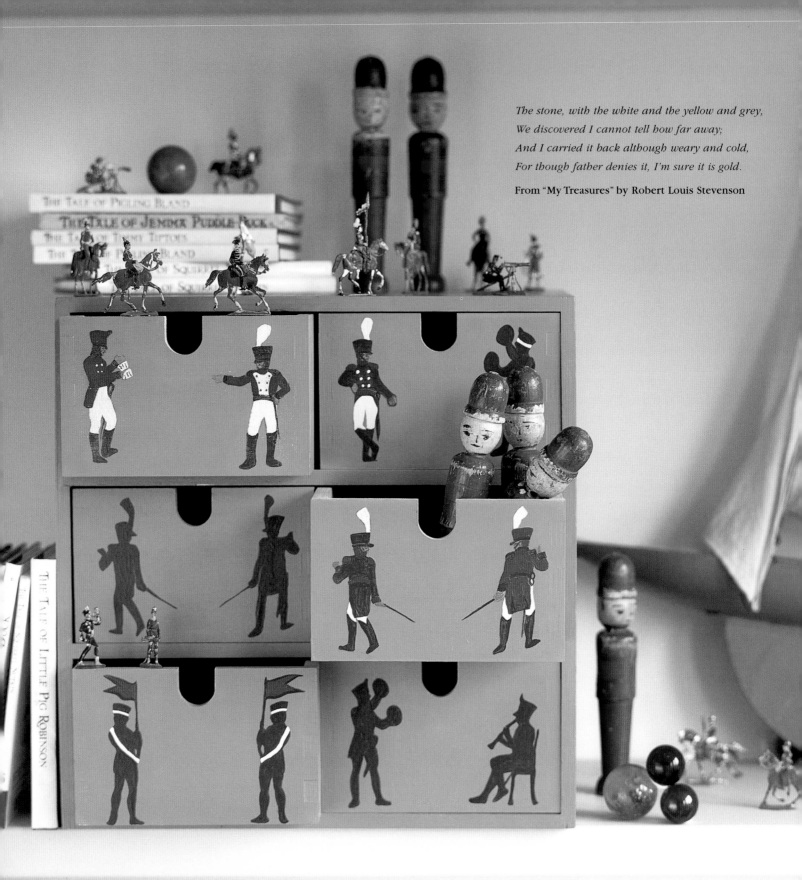

The stone, with the white and the yellow and grey,
We discovered I cannot tell how far away;
And I carried it back although weary and cold,
For though father denies it, I'm sure it is gold.

From "My Treasures" by Robert Louis Stevenson

storing treasures

Children are endearingly receptive to the notion of treasure. The poem opposite, by Robert Louis Stevenson, who seemed to have a direct line to the thoughts of children, perfectly captures the way in which children gather and hoard the oddest objects. A lump of shiny rock bought with spending money in a French market, a gold tassel fallen from the soldier's uniform during the changing of the guard at Buckingham Palace, a vintage football-team badge, collecting cards—these are all treasures, and deserve an appropriate place in which to keep them safe.

This treasure box has used silhouettes taken from an antique book on the militia, decorated in very simple colors. Each drawer has been lined with color photocopies of old military maps.

Alternatively, paint a single soldier inside each drawer. The drawers can easily be taken out of the box and stacked, forming turrets and towers for important battles.

Four little chests all in a row,
Dim with dust, and worn by time,
All fashioned and filled, long ago,
By children now in their prime.

Treasure boxes encourage children to nominate only certain possessions as treasures, especially when so many things seem to come their way. However, a treasure box can also be made with children in mind, but presided over by mother, like "a certain cedar chest, in which Mrs. March kept a few relics of past splendor as gifts for her girls when the proper time came." Decorate a box for each child and fill it with his or her school reports, sports medals, birth-announcement cards, first shoes, and so on. Paint the child's name and birth date on the box and keep it safe until it seems appropriate to hand it over.

Little chests of drawers in varying sizes are very appealing to children. Antique sets of drawers, some with their original worn paint, are sometimes found in flea markets. Some are very characterful and have been made from old fruit crates or cigar boxes. There are also many inexpensive modern boxes and sets of drawers available in stores which can be transformed into magical treasure boxes with a little paint and imagination.

painted treasure box

The transformation of this inexpensive wooden box has been inspired by the delightful vintage pull-along toy on page 8. You can follow the steps given here, but choose your own colors, or you can create a design of your own. Any ordinary household latex paint can be used, both for the base coat and the decorative painting. Here a mixture of latex and acrylic paints have been used. The templates for this design are on page 121; you may need to enlarge or reduce them on a photocopier to get the right proportions for your box, then simply cut out the photocopy to draw around.

materials and equipment

wooden box

fine sandpaper

latex or acrylic paints

brushes

pencil, tracing paper, and scissors

2 soft lint-free cloths

wax

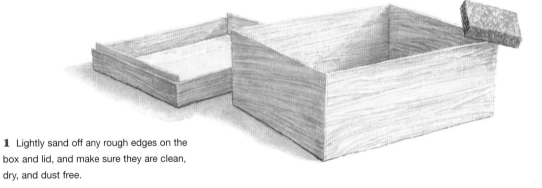

1 Lightly sand off any rough edges on the box and lid, and make sure they are clean, dry, and dust free.

2 Paint the outside of the box with two coats of mid-green flat latex, allowing each coat to dry thoroughly. If you want to paint the inside of the box as well, do it now. It would be a nice idea to paint the name and birth date of the child inside the lid of the box.

3 Lightly sand the painted surfaces with very fine sandpaper and wipe with a cloth.

4 Make a tracing of the templates. Cut them out and lightly pencil the outlines of the little figures and hearts around the box. Draw the edging decoration freestyle around the lid, then either draw or lightly trace the letters on the top. Try to keep pencil markings to a minimum —they are surprisingly difficult to paint over.

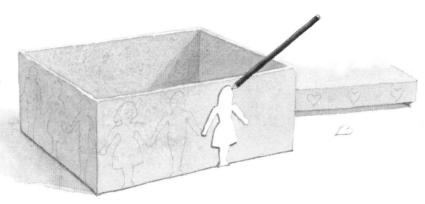

5 Paint the figures, using one color at a time and allowing each layer of paint to dry thoroughly. Paint the paler colors first: you will need two coats when you apply a pale color over a darker color. Enjoy painting the details, and do not feel that you have to stick rigidly to the design. Be brave and add some impromptu details without benefit of prior tracings—they will add charm and personality to the finished box.

6 Once the figures have been painted and are thoroughly dry, lightly sand them using the fine sandpaper. You can do this just to smooth the surface, or you can sand a little bit harder, to break through the layers of paint for a slightly distressed or worn finish.

7 Using a lint-free soft cloth, lightly work wax into the surface of the box, rubbing in one direction so the wax is worked evenly into the paint. Leave for 10–15 minutes. Using another lint-free soft cloth, buff the surface of the box until you have a pleasing waxed finish.

8 If you did not paint the inside of the box, you could line it now with paper or fabric, using an appropriate adhesive.

83

rainy afternoons

One of my favorite childhood memories is of spending a whole rainy-season afternoon with my mother making a relief map of Africa out of flour and water mixed together to make a dough. Of course, I realize now that if we had had the right recipe, we could have baked the dough and painted it different colors. At the time it seemed thrilling enough to pinch out the Atlas Mountains and Rift Valley, where we had been on vacation, and to pour water into little channels carved out for the Niger, the Zambezi, and the Nile rivers. What I treasure is the afternoon spent together, engaged on a matter of great importance.

Children have considerable stamina and tenacity when it comes to seeing a project through to its conclusion. No tea breaks for my husband and I when we made these wooden boats at a rented villa in the south of France with my six-year-old godson and his brother. We

84

These simple wooden boats were made on vacation in France. All you need is three small pieces of wood in varying lengths, the longest of which should ideally be tapered to a point. The three pieces were joined together with a long nail, which also served as a mast. I suspect that there are those with a greater understanding of carpentry and the dynamics of boats, but these floated across the swimming pool quite nicely without sinking and can be sailed in less exotic surroundings back at home.

LE SAUTAIRE I

The general store here was made from plywood, probably in the 1930s. The shelves are raked to provide lots of different ways to arrange miniature foodstuffs, tiny bouquets of flowers in small terracotta pots, and baskets of different berries, nuts, and seeds. On a rainy afternoon it is still a captivating toy with which to play endless games of shops—particularly appealing when the provisions are edible.

one of the best presents you can make for a child is an addition to his or her dressing-up box

used bits of wood pilfered from the owner's shed to construct the boats. Then, under the shelter of an umbrella, the children painted the wood with acrylic paints from a local hardware store.

Even if you do not have your own children, and perhaps especially if this is the case, there are two things you need to entertain young visitors on rainy afternoons. One is a large box that can be made into a shop, little house, theater, ship, or whatever their imagination requires. The other is a hamper of dressing-up clothes. A large wicker basket is a wonderful way of dealing with all those wardrobe and make-up mistakes that you cannot quite bring yourself to throw away. Draped around small children, those scarves, shirts, and old lengths of fabric can get a new lease on life. Children adore dressing up, and one of the best presents you can make for a child is an addition to the dressing-up box. Make a swirling magician's cape in velvet, decorated with appliqué in bright silks. Spend an afternoon creating the most sumptuous crown using cardboard and paste beads.

Remnant boxes are a good source of fabric: small pieces of velvet for a cape, or silk that can be attached to a long run of fabric to make an exotic skirt. Vintage artificial flowers are very inexpensive and look wonderful on little straw hats. Beads, sparkling costume jewelry, and anything with the connotation of treasure will capture the imagination of any child.

generations of women have bonded over an afternoon spent baking, and it is never to early to start—of course, boys like baking, too!

A calm grandmother bakes with her two grandchildren and a small friend. Everyone gets a turn in the mixing bowl. Why not buy a small wicker hamper or basket and fill it with animal cutters, a small rolling pin with hand-painted handles, and a handmade apron? Better still, give it to a child with a little note promising to spend an afternoon baking together.

It's raining, it's cold, and everyone needs cheering up. What better way to spend an afternoon with children than baking? They are so easy to please: a cookie recipe, some edible decorations, and a selection of shaped cutters are all you need.

Baking is an absorbing form of magic for children. Don't even try it if you can't bear the mess. Half the fun is sifting flour everywhere but in the bowl; sticky, buttery fingers and little pieces of pastry smoothing the grain of your kitchen table are unavoidable! The trick is to give each child their own space and utensils, and let everyone have a turn at the mixing bowl. Light handling of the dough is out of the question, so you need a fail-safe but delicious cookie recipe. It is probably a good idea to reserve some dough in case of tragic accidents. Also useful are some shaped cookie cutters, a few tubes of lurid icing, and other edible decorative accoutrements. If you produce a cup of stiff royal icing that you have made earlier, they can spread it on the cookies and paint designs on top with food coloring. Messy, but fun.

These little cut-out dolls are the oldest trick in the world, but they are a lovely way of whiling away an afternoon. Make runs of cardboard dolls and then cut out lots of tiny squares in a variety of fabrics. It might be fun to have a pile of trimmings and buttons as well.

Let each child draw the faces and design their own clothes using the patches. If you are missing a favorite grandchild, why not send her or him a letter with a little packet of paper people and patches as a tiny present?

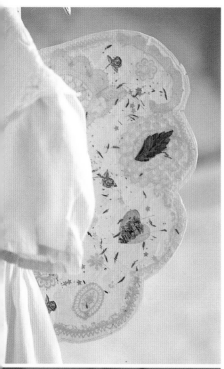

fairy wings

Fairy wings are definitely part of a little girl's capsule wardrobe. Curvy lace edges on old tablecloths or dresses make wonderful edgings, as do paper doilies. Collect tiny leaves from the garden, dried rose petals, or cut out little white paper hearts. The finished wings will be translucent, so keep the design quite delicate. The varnish stiffens the the body of the wings, but it is a good idea to make the final span not much wider than the shoulders of your child, or the wings may start to flop.

materials and equipment

pencil, paper, cardboard for templates (see page 121)

clear plastic sheet

book-binding tissue

weak solution of wallpaper paste

decorations, such as doilies, lace scraps, dried flowers and leaves, paper stars and hearts

glue

oil-based flat-finish varnish

2 equal lengths of thick ribbon

sewing kit

1 Using a photocopier, expand the fairy-wing template (see page 121) to the desired size. Place it on a folded piece of paper, draw around the outline, and cut out the two wing shapes from the paper.

2 Expand the templates for the back panels (see page 121) by the same proportions as the wings. (The tabs should be at least 3 in (8 cm) deep and the same length as the inner edge of the wings.) Draw them on cardboard, then cut out. You need to cut two side tabbed panels and one central strip. These panels provide support for the wings.

3 Place the two paper wings on a flat surface. Lay a sheet of plastic over them (for protection). Cover the area of the wings with a sheet of book-binding tissue. Brush on a layer of wallpaper paste. Repeat with another layer of tissue and paste.

4 Gather together the decorations you are using. You need to work fairly quickly at this stage, while the paste is still wet.

5 Making sure you are working within the outline of the template, arrange your decorations on the wings.

6 Cover with a layer of book-binding tissue. Brush the surface with wallpaper paste, then layer a final piece of tissue over this.

7 Peel the "sandwich" of tissue and decorations off the plastic sheet and hang it up to dry. When dry, replace it over the wing shapes, trace around the outline, and cut out the two separate wings.

8 Machine stitch around the edge of each wing, then stitch three radial lines from the center to the outer edge on each wing. Trim the edges neatly.

9 Stitch or glue (using very strong glue) each wing to one of the tabbed back panels. Then overlap the central areas of the tabs (marked "a"), cover them with the central strip, and again stitch or glue all the pieces securely together. Varnish the wings and leave them to dry.

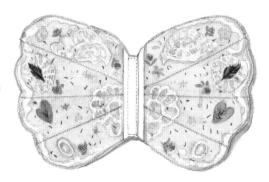

10 Stitch the two lengths of ribbon in place, or punch two holes at the top and the bottom of the back plate and thread the ribbon through.

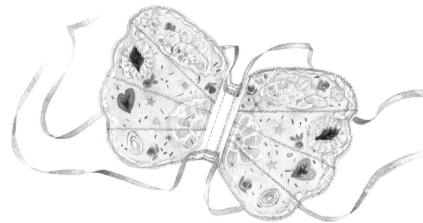

11 Glue scraps of paper and lace to the exposed part of the back panel, allowing pieces of lace to trail down gracefully.

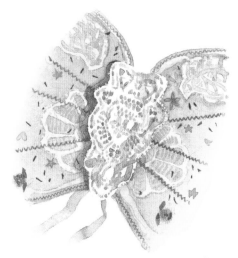

high days & holidays

Annual celebrations and festivals, high days and holidays, mark both the seasons of the year and the unfolding of family life and, in particular, of the lives of the children within the family. Every family marks these occasions in its own way, creating traditions such as the setting out of birthday party tables, transforming the home with colorful handmade decorations, or eagerly opening the numbered doors of homemade advent calendars.

This opulent stocking **(above, left)** has been made from scraps of embroidered textile, velvet, beads, and gold braid, and reflects the theatrical background of the painter who made it. The rust-colored velvet lining makes it all the more pleasurable to delve into in search of presents. The delightfully quirky angels **(above, center and right)** are made from handmade papers and papier-mâché over wire.

holiday

The weeks leading up to Christmas are unbearably exciting for most children: opening the first window on the advent calendar, writing the first draft of the letter to Santa, casting sessions for the school nativity play, the combined delights of glue and glitter.

Children often receive so many presents at Christmas that it is rather nice to try to think of something handmade and different to give, even if it is a small token in addition to something they have actually asked for on their list. Perhaps give each child you know a handmade decoration for each Christmas of their childhood, so that when they are grown up they have a readymade collection of ornaments with which to decorate their own tree. If you are an aunt or godmother, make a special stocking which you fill with little gifts each year and hang at your own house. On the other hand, mothers have a difficult time trying to pull everything together at the holiday season, so a handmade stocking would be a lovely present to receive—all they have to do then is fill it!

holiday stocking

This simple holiday stocking has a pocket for last-minute amendments to the list for Santa Claus. The one in the photograph has been lined, but this is optional, and the steps on these pages do not include instructions for lining the stocking.

1 Using a photocopier, expand the stocking, cuff, heel, toe, and pocket templates (see page 119) at the same proportion to the size required. Our stocking measured 33 in (84 cm) from the tip of the toe to the loop. Cut out all the templates.

materials and equipment

pencil and paper for templates (see page 119)

heavy linen fabric for the body of the stocking

heavy striped cotton fabric (same weight as the linen) for the stocking cuff and the hanging loop

checked or patterned cotton fabrics for the heel, toe and pocket patches

iron-on bonding web

sewing kit

cutting out

from heavy linen:

2 stocking pieces

from striped fabric:

2 cuff pieces

from checked fabric:

1 toe piece and 1 heel piece

2 pocket patches

2 With right sides together, fold the main fabric to a width large enough to hold the stocking template. Pin the template to the fabric, draw around it using a dressmaker's pen, and cut out along the line. Repeat for the cuff. You should now have two stocking pieces and two cuff pieces.

3 Again with right sides together, pin, baste, and sew one cuff piece to each stocking piece to make the front and back of the stocking. Press the seams down.

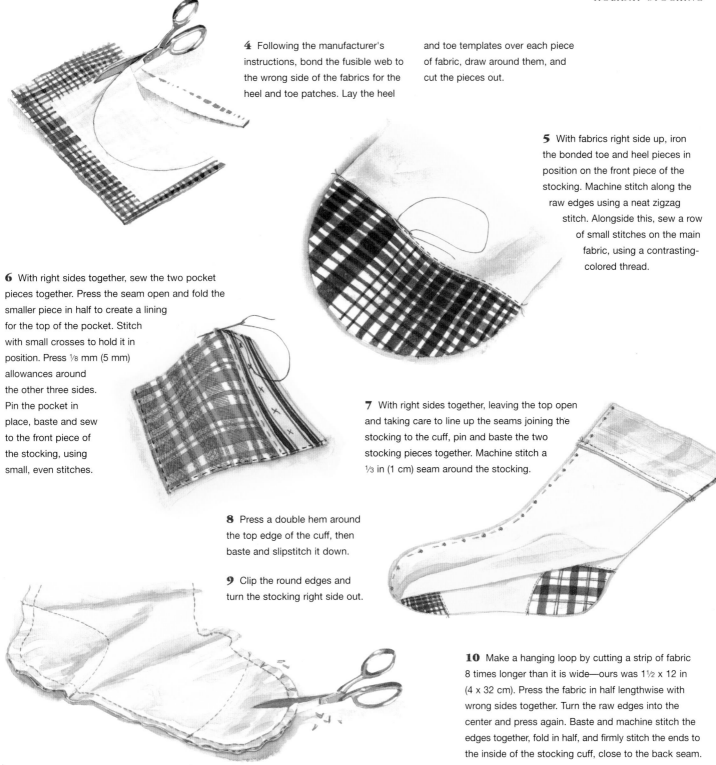

4 Following the manufacturer's instructions, bond the fusible web to the wrong side of the fabrics for the heel and toe patches. Lay the heel and toe templates over each piece of fabric, draw around them, and cut the pieces out.

5 With fabrics right side up, iron the bonded toe and heel pieces in position on the front piece of the stocking. Machine stitch along the raw edges using a neat zigzag stitch. Alongside this, sew a row of small stitches on the main fabric, using a contrasting-colored thread.

6 With right sides together, sew the two pocket pieces together. Press the seam open and fold the smaller piece in half to create a lining for the top of the pocket. Stitch with small crosses to hold it in position. Press ⅛ mm (5 mm) allowances around the other three sides. Pin the pocket in place, baste and sew to the front piece of the stocking, using small, even stitches.

7 With right sides together, leaving the top open and taking care to line up the seams joining the stocking to the cuff, pin and baste the two stocking pieces together. Machine stitch a ⅓ in (1 cm) seam around the stocking.

8 Press a double hem around the top edge of the cuff, then baste and slipstitch it down.

9 Clip the round edges and turn the stocking right side out.

10 Make a hanging loop by cutting a strip of fabric 8 times longer than it is wide—ours was 1½ x 12 in (4 x 32 cm). Press the fabric in half lengthwise with wrong sides together. Turn the raw edges into the center and press again. Baste and machine stitch the edges together, fold in half, and firmly stitch the ends to the inside of the stocking cuff, close to the back seam.

This delightful rabbit **(right)** has been made from felted wool and decorated with simple embroidery in soft colors. Use felt and embroidery to create egg cozies or little purses for individual chocolate eggs.

Easter

Whatever your religious beliefs, the Easter holiday is a great opportunity for family get-togethers. Easter breakfasts were always surprises in our home: there was something magical about finding nests of colored eggs presided over by fluffy chicks, even in deepest Africa!

Create a collection of painted eggs by giving one to a child each Easter of his or her childhood. Or make egg cozies that they can use all year round. Of course, chocolate eggs may be required, but make eager little legs work for them: Easter-egg hunts among the daffodils are childhood memories to treasure. Most importantly, after a breakfast of chocolate and eggs with chick-shaped toast, get out into the countryside and show children all the signs of the changing seasons. The fall before, choose a spot in the yard or set aside a windowbox to plant some early spring flowers, then watch them come out as Easter approaches.

Set an Easter table **(above and opposite)** to welcome the family to breakfast with the colors of sugared almonds rather than customary yellow. Make it a family tradition that everyone receives a hand-painted egg, and keep them

in the family treasure box. Eggs like these are very time-consuming to make, but you can create simpler versions, or just paint boiled eggs with food coloring and stencil simple shapes over the top.

birthdays

Birthdays afford another opportunity for a family to make a fuss of one particular member, creating the tradition of celebration by having special family breakfasts or wonderfully inventive parties. My mother gave the most wondrous children's parties, without benefit of hired venue or entertainment. On my fifth birthday we sat down to tea on the long veranda of our house, and in front of each child was a little card with a hand-colored picture of an animal, the noise of which we were instructed to imitate on the count of three. I can still hear the sounds.

There are so many creative ways in which to make parties great fun for children and adults alike. When children are too little to hunt for treasure, paint huge colorful paper flowers, glue them to sticks, and put them among them flower beds, instructing each small guest to find a flower and bring it back in order to claim a prize. Make tiny little shopping bags with labels for placecards at a birthday party table. Ask everyone to bring their bag to be filled with tiny homemade cookies as they leave.

Involve children in making the food for their birthday party (right and below). If you are feeling really brave, set out a plate of unadorned gingerbread men and women, a selection of decorations, and tubes of colored icing, and allow the guests a free rein to decorate their own.

a childhood punctuated each year with a party filled with color, noise, magic, inventive games, and delicious food is as much of a gift as a present wrapped in paper and ribbon

Children love party bags (right and opposite). If you are giving a small party, make the party bags out of fabric and decorate them with embroidery and stencils or stamps. Stamp a different image on each bag that best reflects each guest, then put the stamp in the bag as a present.

a present for the teacher

A good kind teacher is one of the best gifts a child can have, and it is perhaps a good idea to involve a child in the preparation of something with which to say thank you at the end of term. Surely any teacher would be delighted to receive a tiny jar of jelly to enjoy with breakfast in bed at the end of a long hard term. Making jelly is not difficult. In fact, a basic blackberry jelly is just about the easiest thing in the world to make, and there is something so satisfying about lining up little jars of homemade produce to give as presents. I have a friend who swoons at the mere mention of raspberry jam, so instantly is she transported back to her mother's fruit garden and summer afternoons filled with the indescribably delicious smell of raspberries and sugar. Even if you do not grow or pick the berries yourself, all you need is a pound, and you have enough for a few small jars. If you keep the tiny jars from hotels, your small hoard of berries will stretch even farther. Children love to pick fruit, and as long as you keep them safe from the hot preserving pan, they find the whole process very exciting.

a good kind teacher is one of the best gifts a child can have, so it is fitting to involve a child in the preparation of something with which to say thank you at the end of term

Thoughtful presentation makes gifts all the more special. While you're dealing with the hot jelly, children can be busy making the little labels. Cut little circles of cloth with pinking shears and ask someone with little hands to hold the circles over the lids while you tie some string around the fabric.

Even a bottle of wine can be transformed into a something a little more personal by wrapping it up and adding a homemade decoration. The little bird here has been made by fusing fabric to cardboard, cutting out the shapes for the wing and body, and gluing them together. Tiny bits of foliage and twig from the backyard tied with raffia and a painted heart have been stitched to the bottom of the bird.

create a treasure trove of family memories
with handmade boxes and folders

remembering ...

Children do and say so many extraordinary things that it would be impossible to capture all of them for posterity. Modern technology enables us to record more than our parents could, although I am not sure I do not prefer the soundless flickering images of movie film to the digital perfection of today's videos. It certainly seems to be part and parcel of loving a child that one saves the things he has made, or records the particularly sweet or funny things he has said. There is no doubt that in adulthood, a child who finds all these things recorded in a special book or wrapped in a box that has been handmade to reflect

the treasure consigned to it, will feel that his childhood creations and sayings were extremely precious to his parents.

Families are fascinated by their antecedents, and in creating albums and archives one is not only recording the present, but informing future generations. It is worrying to think that in the future these archives might be DVDs stacked in neat rows on a shelf, the documents scanned in, the objects photographed, the clutter long discarded. How can a video or DVD compare with taking a fragile box down from the attic, brushing off the dust, and finding inside a pair of tiny shoes, with

Keep tiny mementoes of childhood—first teeth, worn leather shoes, a christening bracelet—in a handmade box covered with decorative paper **(opposite, left)**. Make one for each child so they can keep similar things for their own children—so a simple, paper-covered box becomes a precious family heirloom.

Children produce enough artwork to fill a gallery. Keep it safe and neat by making a portfolio **(opposite, right)** for the artwork of each child in the family, using colored photocopies of their work. Bind the collaged pictures together with book-binding tissue and paste, just as for the fairy wings project on pages 90–91.

Rather than putting all your family treasures in the attic, keep a special chest of drawers **(right)**, with perhaps one drawer for each child, in which you keep clothes, artwork, school reports, and other mementos.

The album on these pages has been made by hand, starting with an embroidered tree of life on the cover. Thick pieces of paper are bound into the album, for which a special box has been made. The perfect repository for photographs and anecdotes of childhood and family life, and a wonderful present for anyone who has just had their first child.

This embroidered picture **(above)** was commissioned for a much-loved teacher by Holly's mother. The words are those of the school hymn, and the image of a small girl with long yellow plaits, jumping rope under the large tree by the school gate will be particularly potent for the teacher who spent so much time helping her through her first years at school.

a line of indentations where growing toes pushed against the leather. Family mementos are far more potent when you can hold things that several generations have held. A friend has said she would part with almost anything before letting go of her grandmother's christening robe, in which almost every member of her family born since then has been christened. She has made an exquisite box in which the dress is transported up and down the country as each new member of the family arrives. The dress is charged with connection between the generations of the same family, and is thus so much more than fine cotton and lace. It is extraordinary that an 11-year-old could express so touchingly in the following poem, the desire to hold on to things that remind us of our children's childhood.

Home ain't a place that gold can buy or get up in a minute
Afore it's home there's got t'be aheap a'livin' in it;
Within the walls there's got t'be some babies born, and then
Right there ye've got to 'bring em upt' women good, an' men.
And gradjerly as time goes on ye find ye wouldn't part
With anything they ever used they've grown into yer heart
The old chairs, the playthings, too, the little shoes they wore
Ye hoard; an if ye could ye'd keep the thumbmarks on the door.

"Home Poem" written by an 11-year-old girl in Iowa in 1936.

covered notebook

We all love notebooks: there is such pleasure in having a crisp, blank page in front of us to write on or decorate as we like. The technique for this book is incredibly simple: if you have young relatives coming to visit, you could make the notebook with them, and they could fill it with a diary of their visit. Or simply leave the cover blank so they can choose their own materials and shapes to decorate it. Alternatively, you could make one for each child to take on vacation. Any sort of paper can be used: thick handmade paper is good for photographs, and the finest tissue for dividers. Make a tiny notebook and send it to a child, asking them to write a story for you and send it back!

materials and equipment

good-quality paper for the pages

thick paper for the cover

metal ruler and pencil

box cutter or guillotine

hole punch

ribbon

large darning needle

selection of small pieces of fabric

iron-on bonding web

1 Decide on the size for your notebook. It can be any size, although if you don't have a guillotine, it is hard to make a really uniform block of paper for the inside pages, so you may find it easier to size your notebook according to a pad or pack of ready-cut paper. If you are making a miniature notebook, scissors will be fine for cutting the inside pages.

2 The cover papers are made from thick paper, which is folded back on itself to create a more substantial book. Using a metal ruler and box cutter (or a guillotine), cut two pieces of paper measuring the height of your notebook by twice the width of your notebook.

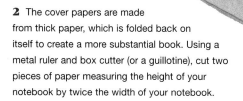

3 Using a metal ruler and pencil, make a clean score halfway across the wrong side of the width of each cover paper. Now fold along the score line so the right side of the paper is showing.

4 If the paper for your inside pages is too large, use a metal ruler and box cutter (or a guillotine) to trim it to the right size.

5 With the back cover on a flat surface, place the inner pages and front cover on top, lining the edges up carefully. The folds on the covers should lie on the outer edge, opposite the spine. Mark the positions for your 4 punched holes along the spine edge of the covers and pages. The covers and pages will probably need to be punched in batches, so take care to keep the holes aligned.

6 Cut your ribbon to a length of approximately 4 times the height of your notebook. Fold it in half lengthwise and thread it through the darning needle. Sew the ribbon through the holes as shown below, beginning by threading down through the third hole from the top.

7 Continue to thread the ribbon, working carefully through the covers and all the pages. Each time you pass through one of the holes, straighten the ribbon so it looks neat and the tension is even.

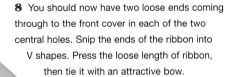

8 You should now have two loose ends coming through to the front cover in each of the two central holes. Snip the ends of the ribbon into V shapes. Press the loose length of ribbon, then tie it with an attractive bow.

9 Decorate the front of the notebook with fabric hearts attached to the paper using bonding web (see page 115).

tools, techniques, & inspirations

Someone once told me that to find inspiration you had to be sure to look around you with your eyes wide open, all the time. Take time to seek out fabrics and treasures that inspire you. Hunt through every button box and basket of lace on the flea-market table. Surround yourself with inspiring treasures, colors, scraps, and cuttings to stimulate your creativity.

When you start work on a piece, gather around you all the things you find most inspiring and pick from them those you wish to use. Make sure your fabric is visible, not tucked away in baskets and boxes. Look for handkerchiefs with pretty scalloped and embroidered edges, spools of old tape with embroidered designs, faded embroidery thread, and packs of mother-of-pearl buttons with their lustrous sheen and lovely shapes.

getting started

I was thrown out of needlework class at the age of 11. Yet again, my basting stitch resembled "dogs' teeth." It was suggested I would fare better in cooking class. I didn't. I remember desperately wanting to be able to sew. Even some years later, I would gaze out of the history Nissen hut across to the needlework hut and feel extremely jealous of the girls who spent a whole year creating exquisite projects. It is still a mystery to me that I earn my living with a needle and thread, but I do know that there has been no training in between. Sewing is easy. You just need to want to make something badly enough to try.

There are two strands to many of the projects in this book: creative and technical. There is nothing particularly creative about making nice piping and sewing straight lines or making a perfect buttonhole, but they are vitally important for a good finish. On the other hand, you can do wonderful embroidery without ever learning anything more than straight stitch and stab stitch. Treat the needle and thread as drawing with a pencil in slow motion, and you will be surprised at how you can suddenly embroider simple shapes. Use the stitches given in this section if you want to, but the best embroidery is that which is imbued with the character and quirks of the person holding the needle. Remember also that once you have gathered a collection of stitches, it is fun to combine them and create your own decorative borders.

The main thing is not to be too ambitious, and to practice on smaller versions of things before heading into a major project. So perhaps before you make a quilt, make a pot holder using log-cabin patchwork techniques and edge it. Perhaps appliqué a heart in the middle and try embroidering some text. If you are successful, you will have a lovely decorative and functional item for your kitchen, and will have gained enough confidence to try the quilt project.

This picture clearly illustrates the effects that can be achieved by applying wax to a finished paint surface. The G and F were originally the same color, but F has had a black-tinted wax applied. The A and B were originally the same yellow, but the B has been waxed with a yellow-tinted wax; the same effect was used on the yellow chair on page 46.

uniform paint, perfectly applied. Use whatever you have on hand to rub the paint back—household sandpaper, the edge of a small knife— and lightly rub the paint back along edges and surfaces that would naturally have been worn. Do not overdo this; it only needs a very light touch to achieve the effect. Finally, consider using colored or neutral waxes to intensify the color of the paint and patinate the surface so that it reflects light and looks more interesting. At any rate, you should always buff your painted surface with a lint-free cloth, which will give a slight sheen and more finished look.

For the projects in this book, we have used latex and acrylic paints, both of which bear some distressing and waxing without running or bleeding. As with sewing, the fun is to experiment and use what you have on hand. I was very struck once by some portraits a friend had done using makeup: she wanted to paint and draw, but had no money for materials, and the results were amazing.

Sewing tools

If you already sew, you will probably have all the equipment you need to make the projects in this book. If you are a complete beginner, you will need to buy or borrow a few things. I would certainly advocate borrowing a sewing machine to see how you like it. Good scissors are vital for cutting straight lines. You need a large pair for cutting fabric, and a small pair with pointed ends for embroidery. I embroider with quilting needles rather than embroidery needles, and my favorite needle of the moment is usually bent into a curve. The point is, use what makes you feel comfortable. If you are going to do a lot of quilting and embroidery, you probably want to use a thimble or little leather stick-on patches to prevent calluses and pinpricks on your middle finger.

A wooden embroidery hoop is useful, especially when you work with filler stitches, such as satin stitch, which need to be very even and smooth. You place the fabric over the smaller hoop and then fit the larger hoop over the fabric, pulling it taut with the help of a screw. Embroidery hoops are inexpensive and can be moved around the fabric if you are working on a larger piece. Don't leave the hoop in place when you stop working or it may distort the fabric.

Chalk and light-sensitive pens are useful for drawing on fabric to help you, especially if you are new to embroidery. It is worth testing the pen on the fabric you plan to use before you start.

Painting wood

Transforming surfaces with paint is extremely satisfying. Old and new wooden boxes can be given a new lease on life with a coat of paint. A good brush is important. I like using the French sash-window brushes with soft bristles that taper into a point. They come in various sizes. A set of ordinary watercolor brushes is also useful for fine work.

Use ordinary household flat latex, which is water-based and easier to create decorative effects with. There are wonderful selections of color to choose from. Sometimes it is effective to use two or three shades around the same tone, and layer them on the wood, sanding the paint back when dry to reveal patches of minutely shaded variations beneath. This painterly approach to decorating wooden surfaces creates a much more interesting and attractive finish than

sewing techniques & stitches

Most of the projects in this book require a basic sewing machine. It is a good idea to get to know what your machine can do. Even the most basic machines have simple embroidery stitches nowadays, with which you can add pattern and texture to plain fabric. Experiment with pieces of cloth to try out stitches and gain confidence. Even if you do not do machine embroidery (it terrifies me!), you can achieve a lovely effect by turning the stitch length right down to buttonhole and moving the fabric around as you sew to create curves and loops with which punctuate a plain fabric surface.

Iron-on stencil

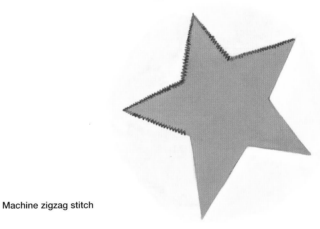

Machine zigzag stitch

Machine appliqué

Hand appliqué on traditional quilts looks wonderful, but is time consuming and cannot withstand the onslaught of twenty-first-century washing machines. An alternative is to use iron-on bonding web. This looks like tracing paper, but one side is slightly textured. On the non-textured side, draw the shape you want to appliqué. Remember that if your shape points in a particular direction, draw it in reverse on the fusible web. So, if you want your bird to point right on the quilt, draw it facing left. This is particularly important for letters and numbers! It is a good idea to make cardboard templates of your favorite shapes so you can simply draw around them and turn them to face in any direction you want.

Having drawn your shape, cut around it, leaving space around the drawn edge. Then place the fusible web, textured side down, on the *wrong* side of the fabric. If using a patterned fabric, you should place the web over the bit of pattern you want to use—for example, a heart over a little rosebud. Fuse the fabric to the web with an iron, following the manufacturer's instructions. Now cut the shape out precisely, peel the paper backing off the fabric, and lay the shape on your background fabric. Again, fuse the two fabrics following instructions. I normally use a thin handkerchief or piece of linen to make sure the iron does not mark the fabrics, particularly when working with fine materials.

Machine appliqué looks best when the stitch is as small as you can manage and the thread matches the fabric very closely. I normally use off-white thread for anything pale, since white tends to be a bit harsh. Select a small-to-medium-width zigzag stitch on your machine, and adjust the stitch length so it is almost on buttonhole. Working very slowly, and in good light, stitch around the shape so you cover the raw edges with the stitching. I find it helpful to start on a straight edge and to slow down on corners, constantly lifting the foot while leaving the needle in place in the fabric. It is a good idea to practice on some simple shapes first.

Keep your machine appliqué stitch as small and neat as possible. You want to have a little bit of space between the stitches—a very fine zigzag as opposed to a solid satin stitch. This gives a more delicate look. Practice on scraps of fabric until you are happy with the quality of your stitching.

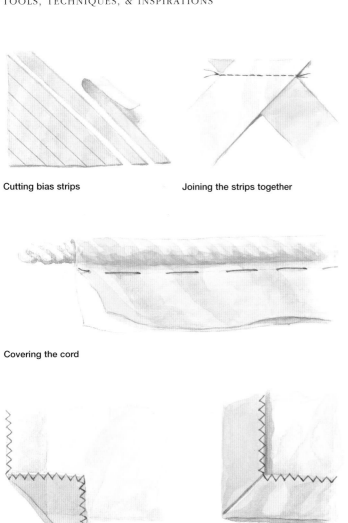

Cutting bias strips

Joining the strips together

Covering the cord

Single hem miter

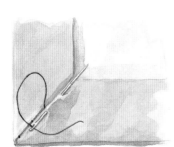

Slipstitch

Stab stitch

Cording

Fabric-covered cord inserted into seams to define the edges (on a pillow, for example) is called cording. Fabric to cover cord is cut "on the bias"—at a 45-degree angle to the grain of the fabric. Cut bias strips approximately 1½-in (3-cm) wide, depending on the thickness of the cord. To join strips, lay them at right angles to each other, with right sides together, then stitch and press the seams open. Lay the cord in the middle of the wrong side of the strip, fold the fabric in half over the cord, and baste, then stitch as close as possible to the cord, starting 2½ in (6 cm) from the end, using a zipper foot.

With the raw edges together, lay cording on the right side of fabric. Again starting 2½ in (6 cm) from the end, stitch as close as possible to the cord, using the correct seam allowance. At corners, clip carefully up to the seam allowance at ¼-in (1-cm) intervals 3 or 4 times. Finish sewing 2½ in (6 cm) from the end of the cording. To join the ends, overlap each end of exposed cord and cut through both pieces. Butt the two ends together and join them with 1 in (2 cm) of micropore tape. To rejoin the fabric, cut both ends at right angles, leaving a seam allowance, stitch together, and finger press the seam flat. Replace the cord in the middle of the bias strip and continue to stitch as above.

Miters

To avoid bulky seams where two hems meet at a corner, you will need a mitre. Press the side hems under, then unfold them. Now fold the corner of the fabric so the fold touches the two crease lines. Fold up each side so they meet in the middle, across the corner—a bit like making a paper airplane. Slipstitch the folded edges.

Slipstitch

This is useful for sewing up, say, a lavender bag or a pillowcover with no opening. You have two folded edges: imagine you are a surgeon sewing up a wound with the aim of an invisible scar! Make the stitches as tiny and neat as possible, and try to catch the threads of the fabric just below the folds rather than on top of them.

Stab stitch

This tiny but strong stitch is used to join layers of fabric together. It can also be used decoratively, to fill an outline or to represent tiny leaves on a tree.

Blanket stitch

A lovely way of decorating an edge, particularly if you are using yarn, blanket stitch is also a decorative stitch in its own right and can be used as an alternative to machine appliqué, although it will not be as durable. It is helpful to imagine the two parallel lines between which you stitch, working from left to right, as a train-track pattern, with the tracks linked along the bottom line.

To start, bring the thread through the fabric toward you on the bottom line and then hold the yarn down below the bottom line with your left thumb while you insert the needle to the right (i.e., the distance you want between your stitches) on the top line. Bring the

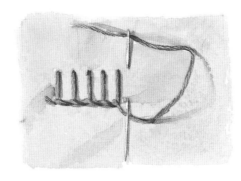

needle back through on the bottom line so the needle is over the held yarn, creating a loop. Continue like this, taking care not to pull the thread too tight. It is best not to have the stitches too far apart.

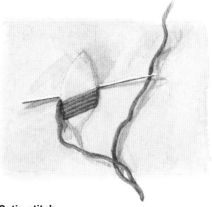

Satin stitch

Traditionally used as a filler stitch, satin stitch is a series of smooth, slightly angled, and closely worked stitches. It is easier if you start at the widest part of the design and work down.

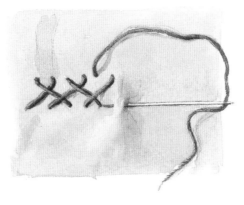

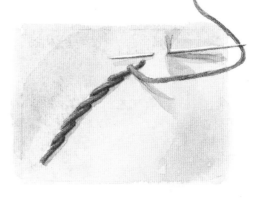

Straight stitch and backstitch

This is the stitch that everyone can do! Bring the needle through to the front of the fabric and insert it in your chosen direction, using a stitch length that you like. It works best when the stitches are not too long or loose. Use backstitch if you want to create a line: bring the needle up through the fabric a stitch length away from the end of the previous stitch, and put the needle back in adjacent to the previous stitch. Repeat. Group these stitches to make flowers and other shapes.

Herringbone stitch

Often found on top of smocking (such as the little red dress on page 57), herringbone stitch is very useful for decorating edges of clothes or seams. Make a long diagonal stitch up and to the right, then insert the needle slightly to the left and bring the thread back across to the right so that you have a large cross with the join toward the top of the cross rather than in the middle. Bring the needle out to the left and repeat, so that the crosses overlap at the bottom this time.

Stem stitch

This is an easy way to make curves and lines, like flower stems. It can also be used as a filler stitch, either in lines or in circles. Begin by indenting the fabric with the tip of the needle to create a working line. Working from left to right, bring the needle to the front of the fabric, slightly to the left of your working line. Now, with the needle angled slightly across the working line, insert it just to the right of the line and bring it through just to the left, a little farther up from the previous stitch.

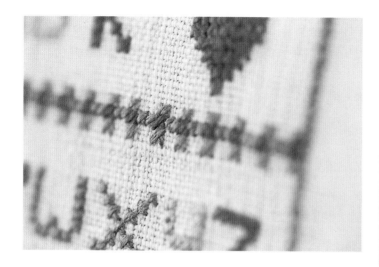

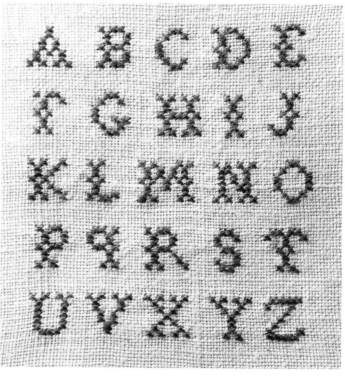

Samplers **(above and right)** were once used to instruct children in the alphabet, which is why there are many charmingly quirky examples. When making a sampler, it is a good idea to use graph paper to sketch your letters, since it is all too easy to make the odd letter a bit wider or longer. The minute alphabet **(right)** has actually been expanded from its original size by about 35 percent and was stitched onto the finest linen.

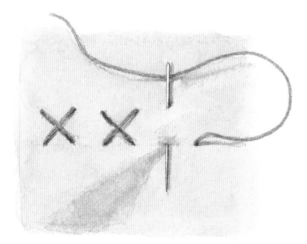

Cross stitch

Begin the cross at the bottom right, working to top left. Then complete the stitch from bottom left to top right. The top diagonal should point the same way on all your stitches for an smooth finish. If you are using plain-weave fabric, scratch the cross positions with your needle tip to guide you.

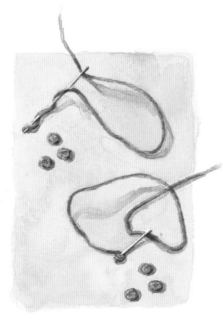

French knots

Bring the needle through to the right side of the fabric. Holding the thread taut, wind it twice around the needle. Keep the thread taut and insert it into the fabric, close to where you brought the thread out. Pull the needle through to the back very carefully, so that the knot slides down the needle and comes to rest on top of the fabric. Just before it touches the fabric, loosen the thread. This stitch does need some practice, but once you have mastered it, you can create some wonderful effects. If it defeats you entirely, cheat by layering two or three tiny straight stitches on top of each other!

Christmas stocking <small>(pages 96–97)</small>

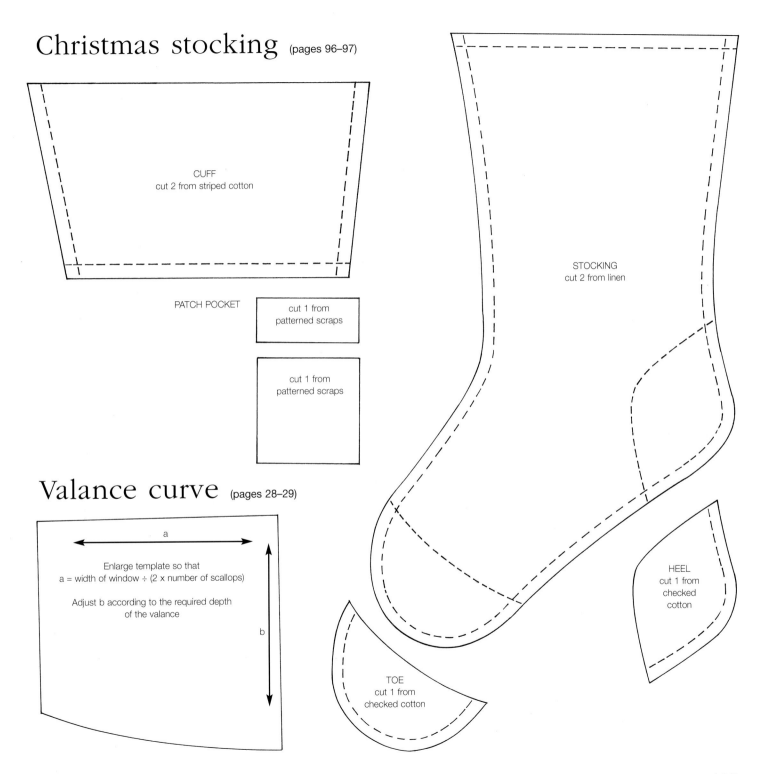

CUFF
cut 2 from striped cotton

PATCH POCKET

cut 1 from
patterned scraps

cut 1 from
patterned scraps

STOCKING
cut 2 from linen

Valance curve <small>(pages 28–29)</small>

a

Enlarge template so that
a = width of window ÷ (2 x number of scallops)

Adjust b according to the required depth
of the valance

b

HEEL
cut 1 from
checked
cotton

TOE
cut 1 from
checked cotton

mister rabbit

(pages 70–73)

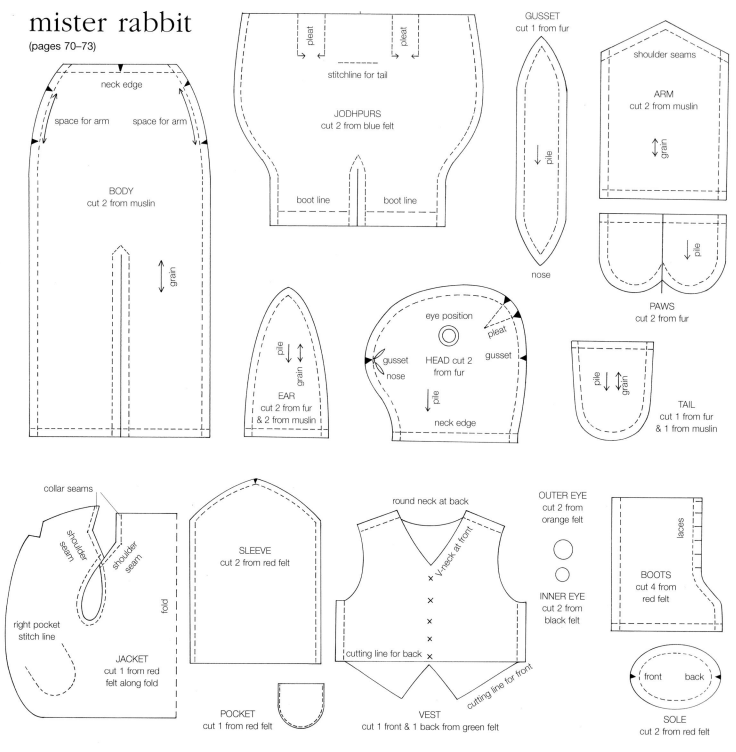

BODY
cut 2 from muslin

neck edge

space for arm   space for arm

grain

JODHPURS
cut 2 from blue felt

pleat   pleat

stitchline for tail

boot line   boot line

GUSSET
cut 1 from fur

pile

nose

ARM
cut 2 from muslin

shoulder seams

grain

PAWS
cut 2 from fur

pile

EAR
cut 2 from fur
& 2 from muslin

pile   grain

HEAD cut 2
from fur

eye position

gusset

nose

gusset

pile

neck edge

TAIL
cut 1 from fur
& 1 from muslin

pile   grain

JACKET
cut 1 from red
felt along fold

collar seams

shoulder seam

shoulder seam

right pocket
stitch line

fold

SLEEVE
cut 2 from red felt

POCKET
cut 1 from red felt

VEST
cut 1 front & 1 back from green felt

round neck at back

V-neck at front

cutting line for back

cutting line for front

OUTER EYE
cut 2 from
orange felt

INNER EYE
cut 2 from
black felt

BOOTS
cut 4 from
red felt

laces

SOLE
cut 2 from red felt

front   back

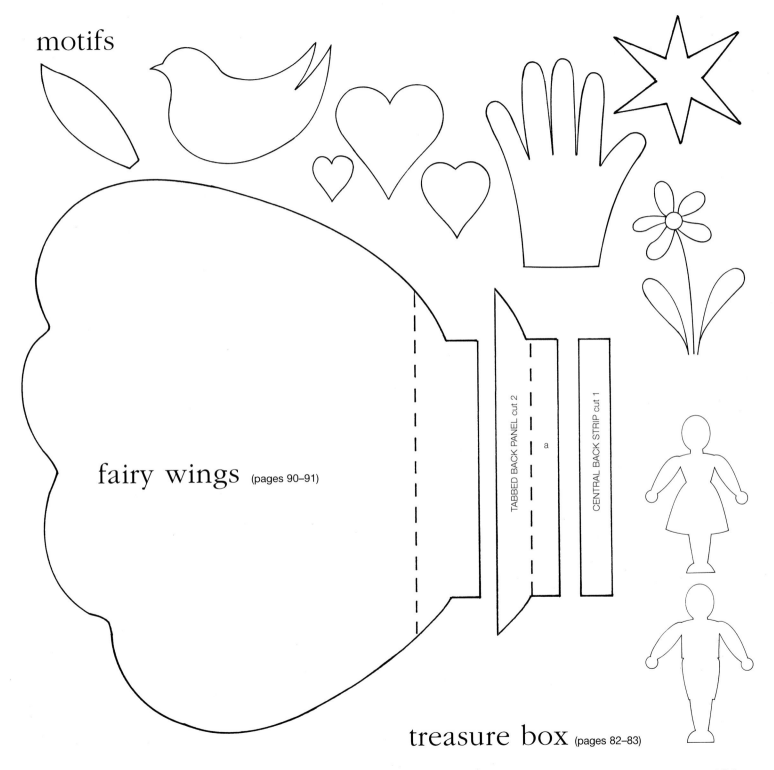

motifs

fairy wings (pages 90–91)

TABBED BACK PANEL cut 2

a

CENTRAL BACK STRIP cut 1

treasure box (pages 82–83)

resources

A Victorian Elegance
P.O. Box 2091
Plant City, FL 33564-2091
800-660-3640
www.victorianelegance.com
*Vintage and antique clothing
and accessories*

ABC Carpet & Home
561-279-7777 for your nearest
store
www.abchome.com
*Home furnishings, fabrics,
and accessories*

American Quilts
P.O. Drawer 200
Upton, KY 42784-0200
877-531-1691
www.americanquilts.com
*Antique, Amish, and custom-made
quilts*

Art Essentials
sbart.essentials.com
info@sbartessentials.com
*Artists' materials and decorative
papers*

The Art Store
1-800-5-GO-ARTS for your nearest
store
www.artstores.com
*Artists' materials and papers;
locations nationwide*

Bloomingdales
1000 Third Avenue
New York, NY 10022
212-705-2000
www.bloomingdales.com
*Department store; 24 locations
nationwide*

Britex Fabrics
146 Geary Street
San Francisco, CA 94108
415-392-2910
www.britexfabrics.com
*Wide variety of ribbons, trims,
and notions*

**The Button Emporium
& Ribbonry**
914 S.W. 11th Avenue
Portland, OR 97205
503-228-6372
www.buttonemporium.com
Vintage and assorted ribbons

Craf-T-Pedlars
1009-D Shary Circle
Concord, CA 94518
877-PEDLARS
www.pedlars.com
Handmade paper and ribbon

Elegant Era's
105 Oak Rim Ct #15
Los Gatos, CA 95032
*Lace, silk, linen, jewelry, and more
from late 1800s to 1940s*

The English Stamp Company
Worth Matravers
Dorset BH19 3JP
England
+ 44 1929 439117 for mail order
sales@englishstamp.com
www.englishstamp.com
*Stamp kits, custom-made stamps,
and nontoxic paints*

Hancock Fabrics
2605A West Main Street
Tupelo, MS 38801
662-844-7368
www.hancockfabrics.com
America's largest fabric store

Hyman Hendler and Sons
67 West 38th Street
New York, NY 10018
212-840-8393
www.hymanhendler.com
Novelty and vintage trims

JAM Paper
800-8010-JAM for your nearest
store
www.jampaper.com
*Papers of all sizes and customized
rubber stamps*

Kate's Paperie
561 Broadway
New York, NY 10012
212-941-9816
Over 40,000 papers

Keepsake Quilting
Route 25B, P.O. Box 1618
Center Harbor, NH 03226-1618
800-865-9458
www.keepsakequilting.com
Quilting fabrics and threads

Laura Ashley Home Store
800-367-2000 for your nearest
store
www.laura-ashleyusa.com
*Floral, striped, checked, and solid
cottons*

Macy's
800-BUY-MACY for your nearest
store
www.macys.com
*Department store; locations
nationwide*

Neiman Marcus
888-888-4757 for your nearest
store
800-825-8000 for mail order
www.neimanmarcus.com
*Department store; 31 locations
nationwide*

Pieces of History Antique Linens
76 Cherry Hollow Road
Nashua, NH 03062
www.tias.com/stores/kayhless
*Sheets, tablecloths, napkins,
pillows, bedspreads, and more*

Potpourri Artist's Supply Inc.

www.potpourri-art.com

18,000 items of art and craft materials to buy online

Reprodepot Fabrics

917 SW 152nd Street

Burien, WA 98166

www.reprodepotfabrics.com

Reproduction vintage fabrics

The Ribbon Club

P.O. Box 699

Oregon House, CA 95962

530-692-3014

www.theribbonclub.com

Ribbons, trims, and tassels

The Ribbonerie Inc.

191 Potrero Avenue

San Francisco, CA 94103

415-626-6184

www.theribbonerie.com

Extensive collection including wired, grosgrain, metallic, and velvet

Tinsel Trading Co.

47 West 38th Street

New York, NY 10018

212-730-1030

Vintage to contemporary trims

ONLINE RESOURCES

www.curioscape.com

Over 40,000 addresses of stores selling antiques, including textiles and vintage clothing throughout the country

www.ebay.com

Internet auctions; every category of merchandize represented

www.fleamarketguide.com

Listings of flea markets held throughout the country

www.marybethtemple.com

Linens from the Victorian era through the 1950s; vintage fabrics and trims

www.vintagefiberworks.com

Vintage clothing, accessories, fabrics, and home decor

www.tias.com

Vast selection of antiques and collectibles, including textiles

FLEA MARKETS

Alameda Swap Meet

South Alameda Boulevard

Los Angeles, CA 90021

213-233-2764

Seven days a week from 10 a.m. to 7 p.m. year round, 400 vendors

Brimfield Antique Show

Route 20

Brimfield, MA 01010

413-245-3436

www.brimfieldshow.com

Brimfield is renowned as the outdoor antiques capital of the world; show held for a week in May, July, and September

Denver Indoor Antique Market

1212 South Broadway

Denver, CO 80210

303-744-7049

Open seven days a week

Merriam Lane Flea Market

14th and Merriam Lane

Kansas City, KS 66106

913-677-0833

Open-air market where estates are bought and sold; weekly in spring and summer from 7 a.m. until dark

Ruth's Flea Market

Highway 431

Roanoke, AL 36274

334-864-7328

Over 300 booths selling collectibles; Wednesdays and Saturdays

Traders Village (Houston)

Eldridge Road

Houston, TX 77083

713-890-5500

Largest marketplace on the Texas Gulf coast, with over 800 dealers and over 60 acres of bargains. Saturdays and Sundays

Artists, designers, and businesses whose work has been featured in this book:

Key: ph=photographer a=above, b=below, r=right, l=left, c=center.

Vanessa Arbuthnott

Fabrics:

www.vanessaarbuthnott.co.uk

Holiday lets: www.thetallet.co.uk

Pages 22c&r, 32, 33a, 34r, 35, 40, 44, 54, 64r, 65, 66, 68, 80l, 81r, 111l

Emma Bowman Interior Design

+44 20 7622 2592

emmabowman@yahoo.co.uk

Pages 5, 8b, 9b, 12–19, 23c, 25b, 42a, 58r, 59c, 60, 61c&r, 69, 76l, 77, 89, 92r& 93l, 101l, 103l, 128

Liz Crowther

Decorative painter

+44 7771 711966

Pages 78, 79, 88, 92c, 98, 99

Caroline Dorling

Papier mâché and wood turning

Flint House

41 High Street

Lewes BN7 2LU, UK

Pages 94c, 94r

Hoggy's Antiques Toys & Textiles

at Sharland & Lewis

(see below for address)

Pages 84–85

jwflowers.com
Unit E8 & 9
1–45 Durham Street
London SE11 5JH, UK
+44 20 7735 7771
+44 20 7735 2011 (fax)
jane@jwflowers.com
www.jwflowers.com
Pages 7, 8a, 52, 53l, 55, 74, 75

Penny Menato
Naif Ideas
Rag dolls and decorative
accessories
22 Park Place
Cheltenham GL50 2QT
UK
www.naifideas.com
Page 32

Sharland & Lewis
52 Long Street
Tetbury GL8 8AQ, UK
+44 1666 500354
www.sharlandandlewis.com
Pages 8–9a, 10, 11b, 32, 33b, 34l,
40, 41r, 56, 66

Victor Stuart Graham
Hand made driftwood boats
Tichbourne Studios
18 Tichbourne Street
Brighton BN1 1UR, UK
+44 1273 203168
Page 40

Kim Sully
Handmade collage boxes
+44 1483 579652 by appointment
Page 104

Olga Tyrwhitt
Textile artist
Courses available
tyrwhitt@ntl.world.com
Pages 32, 33a

Jane Wellman
A hand crafter of teddy bears
G-rumpy bears
33 Strafford Road
Barnet EN5 4LR, UK
+44 20 8275 0693
Page 42b

Jessica Zoob
Artist
+44 1273 478634
www.jessicazoob.com
Pages 1, 3, 4, 24, 25a, 35, 39, 43,
47r, 58l, 90l, 94l

Caroline Zoob
Textile artist and interior design
For commissions please contact:
+44 1273 479274
Caroline Zoob's work is also
available at:

Caroline Zoob
33 Cliffe High Street
Lewes
East Sussex BN7 2AN
+44 1273 476464 (shop & mail
order)
www.carolinezoob.com
Handmade collectables

credits

All photographs by Caroline Arber
Key: ph=photographer a=above, b=below, r=right, l=left, c=center.

Endpapers cut out dolls made by Greta (70+), Ana (7) and Katerina Zoob (4); page 1 artist Jessica Zoob's family home in London; 2 Sophie Eadie's family home in London, patchwork quilt and vintage toys, Housepoints; cushions Caroline Zoob Design; 3 & 4 artist Jessica Zoob's family home in London 5 Emma Bowman Interior Design, vintage wooden toys from Housepoints; 6 Caroline Zoob, all items from Housepoints; 7 Paul Balland & Jane Wadham of jwflowers.com's family home in London, doll and cup loaned by Katerina Zoob (4); 8a Paul Balland & Jane Wadham of jwflowers.com's family home in London vintage wooden toy from Housepoints; 8b Emma Bowman Interior Design vintage wooden shop and contents from Housepoints; 8–9a Sharland & Lewis; 9b Emma Bowman Interior Design; 10 & 11b Sharland & Lewis; 12–19 Emma Bowman Interior Design all work by Caroline Zoob – 18 all toys sourced by stylist, cushion Caroline Zoob, quilt Housepoints; 22l Caroline Zoob; 22c&r the Arbuthnott family's house; 23l Caroline Zoob; 23c Emma Bowman Interior Design; 23r quilt from Housepoints; 24 & 25a artist Jessica Zoob's family home in London, patchwork quilt Housepoints; 25b Emma Bowman Interior Design, blind designed and made by Caroline Zoob; 26–28 Caroline Zoob; 30l quilt by Caroline Zoob; 30r quilt from Housepoints; 31 Caroline Zoob; 32 & 33a the Arbuthnott family's house near Cirencester designed by Nicholas Arbuthnott, interior design & fabrics by Vanessa Arbuthnott, patchwork blanket by Olga Tyrwhitt, wooden horse Sharland and Lewis, rag doll Naif Ideas; 33b Sharland & Lewis; 34l Sharland & Lewis, blanket embroidered by Caroline Zoob; 34r & 35 the Arbuthnott family's house near Cirencester designed by Nicholas

Arbuthnott, interior design & fabrics by Vanessa Arbuthnott, patchwork quilt on pram by Jessica Zoob; 39 artist Jessica Zoob's family home in London; 40 the Arbuthnott family's house near Cirencester designed by Nicholas Arbuthnott, interior design & fabrics by Vanessa Arbuthnott, eiderdown Sharland and Lewis, model boat Victor Stuart Graham, Samplers Carla Marx, Painting Rose Arbuthnott; 41l Sophie Eadie's family home in London, cushions and quilts from Housepoints, doll's wicker crib from Pure Country; 41r Sharland & Lewis, rabbit from Lizzie's; 42a Emma Bowman Interior Design, embroidery by Caroline Zoob; 42b Sophie Eadie's family home in London, G-rumpy bear by Jane Wellman, cushions by Caroline Zoob; 43 artist Jessica Zoob's family home in London, vintage toys, cushion and patchwork quilt from Housepoints; 44 the Arbuthnott family's house, vintage French fabric from Housepoints; 46&47l Caroline Zoob; 47r artist Jessica Zoob's family home in London, chair and table from Housepoints; 48 Caroline Zoob; 52 & 53l Paul Balland & Jane Wadham of jwflowers.com's family home in London; 53r Caroline Zoob; 54 the Arbuthnott family's house; 55 Paul Balland & Jane Wadham of jwflowers.com's family home in London; 56 Sharland & Lewis; 58l artist Jessica Zoob's family home in London, fairy dress and wings by Caroline Zoob; 58c Housepoints; 58r Emma Bowman Interior Design; 59l Caroline Zoob; 59c Emma Bowman Interior Design; 59r Caroline Zoob; 60 Emma Bowman Interior Design; 61l Caroline Zoob; 61c&r Emma Bowman Interior Design; 62–63 Caroline Zoob, Barbie's loaned by Wilson; 64l Sophie Eadie's family home in London; 64r, 65 & 66 the Arbuthnott family's house near Cirencester designed by Nicholas Arbuthnott, interior design & fabrics by Vanessa Arbuthnott, all vintage toys Housepoints and Sharland & Lewis; 67l Housepoints; 67r Caroline Zoob; 68 the Arbuthnott family's house near Cirencester designed by Nicholas Arbuthnott, interior design & fabrics by Vanessa Arbuthnott; 69 Emma Bowman Interior Design, quilt and animals from Housepoints; 70 & 73 Housepoints; 74 & 75 Paul Balland & Jane Wadham of jwflowers.com's family home in London, vintage farm Housepoints; 76r Caroline Zoob; 76l & 77 Emma Bowman Interior Design, all items stylist's own; 78–79 Caroline Zoob, soldier treasure box painted by Liz Crowther, antique tin soldiers from Housepoints; 80l & 81r the Arbuthnott family's house, chicken box painted by Caroline Zoob; 80r & 81l Housepoints, treasure box painted by Caroline Zoob; 82 Caroline Zoob; 84–85 Hoggy & Mark Nicholl's home in Wiltshire, decorator John Nurmington, Malmesbury; 86–88l & 89 Emma Bowman Interior Design, apron Caroline Zoob, rolling pin handles painted by Liz Crowther; 88r Caroline Zoob; 90l artist Jessica Zoob's family home in London, fairy dress and wings designed and made by Caroline Zoob; 92l Housepoints, Christmas angel by Caroline Zoob; 92c Caroline Zoob, eggs painted by Liz Crowther; 92r & 93l Emma Bowman Interior Design; 94c&r Caroline Zoob, Christmas fairies by Caroline Dorling; 94l & 95 Housepoints, Christmas stocking made by Jessica Zoob; 96 stocking by Caroline Zoob; 98–99 Caroline Zoob, eggs painted by Liz Crowther, knitted blanket Small Acorns, felt rabbit Lizzie's; 101l Emma Bowman Interior Design; 102 & 103r Caroline Zoob; 103l Emma Bowman Interior Design; 104 Caroline Zoob, handmade box by Kim Sully; 108 Caroline Zoob; 111l the Arbuthnott family's house; 111c Caroline Zoob; 112–114 Caroline Zoob; 128 Emma Bowman Interior Design.

Quotations

p17: *The Hooked Rug*, Anonymous, *Old-time Tools and Toys of Needlework* by Gertrude Whiting, 1928. p23: *The Six Bullerby Children* by Astrid Lindgren. London: Methuen, 1963. Reproduced by permission of Egmont. p25: *Family Art* by Philip Pacey. Copyright Philip Pacey. Polity Press, in association with Basil Blackwell, 1989. Reproduced by permission of Philip Pacey. I am grateful to Philip Pacey for writing *Family Art*, a book that anyone wondering what making a "home—in a world" is all about should read. p30: *A Child's Garden of Verses* by Robert Louis Stevenson, 1885. p34: *The Meaning of Things: domestic symbols and the self* by Mihaly Csikszentmihalyi and Eugene Rochberg-Halton. Quoted in *Family Art* (ibid). p 42: *The Standard Book of Quilt Making and Collecting* by Marguerite Ickis. New York: Dover Publications 1960. Reproduced by permission of Dover Publications. p59: *A Child's Garden of Verses* by Robert Louis Stevenson, 1885. p75–76: *Our Mutual Friend* by Charles Dickens, 1865. p76, 77, and 78: *A Child's Garden of Verses* by Robert Louis Stevenson, 1885. p80: *Little Women* by Louisa May Alcott, 1868. p107: *Home Poem* written in a scrap book by an 11-year-old girl in Iowa in 1936. Quoted in *Family Art* (ibid).

The Author has made every effort to secure permission for works in copyright. The Publisher will be happy to amend any errors or omissions in future editions of the book.

index

Page numbers in *italics* refer to
illustrations and captions

thank you to ...

Caroline Arber for her beautiful photographs and unfailingly kind and generous support of my work.

Melanie Osborne for keeping everything going at home, running the Christmas mail-order business singlehandedly, and for her creative, versatile, and, above all, cheerful help on shoots.

Everyone at Ryland Peters & Small, especially Sally Powell, Emily Westlake, Sophie Bevan, and Alison Starling.

Charlotte Palmer, Christine Gilsenan, and Lela Sisauri for their beautiful stitching and help in realising many of the projects.

Elizabeth Falla for binding the album on pages 106–7 so exquisitely.

Greta, Ana, and Katerina Zoob and Isabel Bowman for agreeing to appear in this book

All the people, grown up and little, who loaned their childhood treasures for use in this book.

Emma Bowman and Vanessa Arbuthnott not only for allowing us to photograph their homes but for their kind hospitality.

Last but not least, my parents, who gave me more childhood treasures than I could list in this book.